EVERYDAY CRISIS MANAGEMENT

WHAT PEOPLE ARE SAYING ABOUT
EVERYDAY CRISIS MANAGEMENT

"Dr. Friedman's book reveals the unwavering compass used by emergency physicians to navigate the seas of crisis in an increasingly complex and chaotic world."

Susan Nedza MD MBA FACEP
Board of Directors, American College of Emergency
Physicians

"Every entrepreneur *must* learn to think like an emergency physician."

Gary Hoover MBA, Board of Directors, Hoovers Inc.

"Friedman teaches all of us regular folks how to deal with the sudden and unexpected crises that challenge our integrity and change our lives."

Jeff Hardy, President, Healthcare Enterprise
Development Services

"Down to earth, realistic, evidence based advice. Read this and learn the essential principles for coping on the job, at home, or wherever you are."

Anita Young MEd. RPh.
Director of Continuing Education,
Massachusetts College of Pharmacy

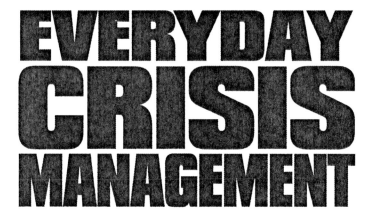

EVERYDAY CRISIS MANAGEMENT

HOW TO THINK LIKE AN
EMERGENCY PHYSICIAN

MARK FRIEDMAN, M.D.

For information contact the author at:
4305 Lonetree Ct.
Naperville, IL 60564

FIRST EDITION   9/11/2002

Published by First Decision Press
Naperville, IL

ISBN 0-9718452-0-4

TABLE OF CONTENTS

WHY YOU SHOULD READ THIS BOOK

Anyone who can learn to think critically and rapidly and then act decisively - like an emergency physician - will gain a competitive edge. This applies in business, in society at large and in your personal life. Fortunes have been made, lives saved and history transformed by individuals utilizing the principles revealed in this book. The difference between success or failure, between triumph or defeat, between life or death often hinges on the ability to change the odds in your favor. Once you read this book, learn its lessons, practice and apply them, you will become consistently more successful than you were before.

ACKNOWLEDGMENTS

Many people over the years have provided me with guidance, opportunity and encouragement. They include my wife Mary, my parents Roslyn and Melvin, my teachers, friends and colleagues in emergency medicine. Thank you all.

I would like to specifically thank Steve and Marla Friedman, Claude and Anita Young and Debbie Friedman for help with proofreading and revision of the initial draft. Thanks go to Gary Hoover for encouragement and help in the publication process.

Special thanks also to all those who contributed the stories and vignettes used to illustrate the principles of crisis management, including Robert Andrews, Brett Galloway, Tony Giancarlo*, Lori Hermesdorf, Richard Murdock, Delia Pachinko*, Dr. John Peltin*, Randall Still*, Katherine Thoreau*, Dr. Joseph Waeckerle, Dr. Les Waal and Dr. Donald Walsh.

Thanks to Alan Friedman, Dr. Richard Westfall and Dr. Joseph Ornato for eye witness accounts of the events of September 11.

I would like to acknowledge the American College of Emergency Physicians, the Federal Emergency Management Agency (FEMA), the Insurance Institute for Highway Safety and the National Transportation Safety Board (NTSB) as sources of useful technical and historical crisis management related information.

FOREWORD

On September 11, 2001 as I labored on the second draft of this book, the world changed. An unspeakably horrible series of terrorist attacks in New York and Washington DC caused the deaths of thousands of Americans and shook the very foundations of the nation. This terrible event grabbed the attention of the entire world and, in the worst possible way, fulfilled the prophesy made in chapter 3 that, "A crisis will occur."

The next day I reported to my clinic job at O'Hare Airport but there was nothing to do. The airport was closed amid tight security. I saw only one patient in seven hours. Like millions of Americans I wondered what, if anything, I could do. Then I realized that by rapidly completing this book I might help others discover what to do. Over the course of several days I gathered as much information as possible on the crisis of September 11 and integrated it into the framework of the book. I completed my redraft by working continuously and hope to publish it in time to do some good.

INTRODUCTION

W hen I began the practice of Emergency Medicine some 20 years ago it did not occur to me that I was practicing crisis management. The multitude of acute and chronic medical cases brought in every day seemed to be individual patients with individual problems. Later, as Chief of Emergency Medicine at a big city teaching hospital, I was involved in disaster planning and management. The idea that the way we managed patients in the emergency room had broad applicability gradually began to take shape as I unconsciously applied these basic concepts of "crisis management" to disaster planning as well as my own personal and business crises.

Crisis management has been popularized for some time in the business arena and there are several books focused on the topic of crisis in business. Managing and teaching others to manage crisis situations and the shifting business paradigms of large corporations is a veritable cottage industry in this country. The Tylenol poisonings of 1986 and the Firestone tire recall of 2000 are two examples of business crisis we will discuss later in this book.

Medical management of both individual and widespread, population based, calamities dates back to antiquity. Epidemics such as the bubonic plague or "Black Death" of the middle ages, smallpox, polio and more recently HIV (AIDS) come readily to mind.

Disaster management, relating to both natural and man-made incidents, has an equally long history. Innumerable wars, fires, floods, famines and earthquakes have occurred from time immemorial. Disaster management is even mentioned in the Bible.

Personal crisis is as old as mankind. Each individual in his or her private life will be forced to deal with multiple crises of personal, group and societal dimensions.

This book offers a unique new approach to crisis management from the vantage-point of emergency medicine. Based on this crisis-tested paradigm we are able to collect and organize wisdom from various disciplines into the framework of crisis management. From this broad experience basic principles can be distilled and clarified. Utilizing these principles, crisis management techniques will be developed, that can be applied by the reader to societal, organizational and personal crisis situations.

The reader will be introduced to techniques utilized every day by emergency physicians to manage crisis. While you should not expect to become an expert crisis manager simply by reading this book, you will become thoroughly acquainted with the skills and strategies involved. It is only through constant application and practice that these skills will become honed to the point that the management of crisis becomes routine.

All of the case histories in this book are real. They are events of which I have either first-hand knowledge or an account from known and reliable observers. In my wildest imagination I could not have invented stories with the power and gripping details of these real life situations. Some of the names (as indicated by an asterisk*) and minor details have been changed to protect privacy and confidentiality.

As you read "Everyday Crisis Management" you will learn about the inevitability of crisis and how to recognize it when it occurs. The book explains how to predict crisis and that prevention is sometimes possible. It goes on to help you prepare and train for the crisis you cannot prevent and then to manage it when it occurs. Crisis management skills are defined, explained and illustrated by example. You will first learn to plan, prepare and train, next to assess, decide and act.

The exercises are part of the learning process. You will not derive maximum benefit from your reading unless you complete them. If you decide to read the entire book first, without doing the exercises, you are well advised to go back, reread and complete them.

INTRODUCTORY NOTE:

While emergency medicine professionals prefer the term "Emergency Department" I have chosen to use the more commonly known term "ER" at the suggestion of my lay reviewers, who said that most readers would not be familiar with the designation, "ED". I trust my colleagues will forgive me. Likewise, in the interest of readability, all pronouns not referring directly to a specific person are designated in the male gender for purposes of readability and convention. The reader may substitute she, or she or he, based on his or her preference.

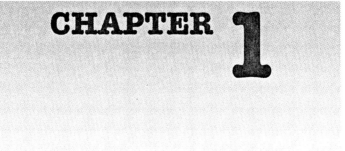

CHAPTER 1

CRISIS

Doctor, the next patient is a 25-year-old male with chest pain."

The nurse's voice held a sense of urgency as she slid the new chart right under my nose, on top of the one I was reading.

"Chest pain isn't usually a serious problem in a 25-year-old," I said, somewhat annoyed but getting up to see the patient. As I entered the room I noticed the nurse had connected the patient to the cardiac monitor, a sign she was indeed taking the patient's complaint seriously.

"Good morning, I'm Dr. Friedman. How are you feeling today?"

"Not too good doc. I feel like my chest is being squeezed in a vise."

The young man looked pale. He was sweating profusely. Beads of perspiration ran down his forehead. The skin under his gown was dripping wet. I held his wrist to take the pulse and noted he felt cold and clammy. The strong odor of tobacco was on his breath.

"How long have you been having this pain?"

"It started when I got on the Mass Pike, about 2 hours ago."

"How bad is it on a scale of one to ten, if ten is the worst pain you've ever had?"

"This is a ten doc."

I looked at his sallow face over the rim of my glasses. He had just driven the length of Massachusetts, over a hundred miles, with crushing chest pain.

The nurse had slipped back into the room and was standing expectantly to one side. "Let's start an IV. Put him on O2. Give him two baby aspirin, a sublingual nitroglycerin and five milligrams of morphine IV push. We need an EKG stat. Draw cardiac enzymes and admitting bloodwork."

I continued taking my history as I examined the patient. He was a 2 pack a day smoker but denied cocaine or other drugs. No personal history of heart disease, diabetes, or hypertension. He did not know his cholesterol level. His brother was diabetic and his father had died suddenly at the age of 49. As I listened to his heart I heard an extra beat and glanced at the cardiac monitor.

"Lidocaine 100 milligrams IV. Then hang a drip at 2 milligrams a minute."

"Doctor would you like to wait for the EKG? The technician is on the way."

"No. Do it now."

As the lidocaine was going in the patient stiffened. His eyes rolled back in their sockets. Then he shook all over, in a brief seizure and lost consciousness. At first I feared a drug reaction, but one look at the cardiac monitor gave the explanation. He was in ventricular fibrillation. His heart had stopped.

"Call a code! Charge the defibrillator, 200 joules."

The charging defibrillator whined as the code team rushed into the room. The patient's gown was ripped off and gel covered paddles were pressed down onto his chest.

"All clear. Shock."

The patient's arms jumped along with an audible jolt as the defibrillator discharged. The cardiac monitor tracing went blank and then reappeared. He was still in V-Fib arrest.

"Charge it again, 300 Joules. Get the intubation tray and a number 8 ET tube."

The room was buzzing now with action. EKG leads were going on. The lidocaine drip was mixed and hung. The intubation tray was brought out.

"All clear. Shock."

Another jolt. The monitor tracing cleared again, but this time came back with a regular, though rapid, rhythm.

"Call cardiology. Let's intubate."

Lifting the patient's tongue and jaw with a shiny steel laryngoscope to reveal his airway, I slid the breathing tube between his vocal cords. Blood was drawn for tests. A portable chest X-ray was done right there in the code room. A suite was reserved in the cardiac surveillance unit. The patient was whisked to the cardiac cath lab where the cardiologist discovered a blood clot in one of his major coronary arteries and dissolved it with TPA, a clot-busting drug.

I was already on to the next patient. At the time it didn't occur to me to think of this as crisis management.

WHAT CONSTITUTES A CRISIS?

The dictionary definition of **crisis** is, "A crucial turning point in the progress of an affair or series of events." In reference to medical applications crisis can be defined as, "Any sudden or decisive change in the course of a disease, favorable or unfavorable." One interesting element of this definition is that crisis is not necessarily a bad thing. It may be a radical change for good as well as bad. Along similar lines is the Chinese concept that crisis may hold the seeds of opportunity.

You are all familiar with examples of crisis in a negative sense: war, natural disaster, sudden shifts in business fortunes, as well as personal crisis situations such as divorce, severe illness, or death of a loved one. How many of you however, recognize such positive turning points as marriage, recovery, the birth of a child, a major promotion, success in an important project, or a business opportunity, as a crisis situation? Think for a moment about a negative personal crisis you have faced. Alternately recollect some positive crisis or turning point in your life.

It is important to understand that certain key elements exist in many, if not all, crisis situations. By recognizing that a given situation represents a crisis and by careful analysis and persistent application of certain basic principles, the reader can tip the odds in his favor and often produce more positive results.

The main time elements of a crisis include:

PRE-CRISIS
CRISIS
RESOLUTION / PRECRISIS

The **pre-crisis** phase is everything leading up the occurrence of the actual crisis itself. This is the time during which the seeds of crisis are sown. It should be used to make ready for the coming crisis. The **crisis** phase which follows is by definition an acute event. After the crisis is over you have the **crisis resolution** phase. This is a time to evaluate the crisis and your response to it. As you will see, it is also the time to begin preparing for the next crisis.

The skills you need to learn include:

RECOGNITION
PREDICTION
PREVENTION
PREPARATION AND TRAINING
EVENT MANAGEMENT
EVALUATION

In this chapter you will learn to recognize a crisis when it occurs. Subsequent chapters will deal with additional skills.

CRISIS RECOGNITION

How do you **recognize** a crisis situation? In the acute phase it's often fairly straightforward. It grabs your undivided attention. Often there are physical signs and symptoms. You get that sick or empty feeling in the pit of your stomach. Your heart rate quickens. You may feel hot and flushed, or cold and weak kneed.

Let's posit some real life examples. You step into an elevator late at night in your apartment building. You press the button for your floor. As the door closes you turn and look up, right into the barrel of a 38-caliber revolver. Do you recognize this as a crisis situation? You bet your life. There is no problem identifying a crisis here. Your heart is "in your throat." Your legs are shaking. Your voice trembles. Physiologically you are experiencing a "fight or flight" response. Intellectually you have immediately recognized you are in a very dangerous situation.

What difference does it make if you consciously label this event a crisis? The answer is that once you have finished this book you will be equipped with an intellectual skill set that should help you to better react to this or any other crisis.

Let's accept the assumption that the identification of some event as a crisis will aid you in its management. Why should it be at all difficult to identify a crisis? You certainly had no difficulty identifying the 38-caliber crisis just discussed. The answer is that some crisis situations are not so "in your face" obvious.

Here is another example. You have just had a disagreement with your spouse. This is only the most recent of many. Is this a crisis? Perhaps it is. How can you tell? Refer back to the definition of crisis: "A crucial turning point in the progress of an affair or series of events." Most people would agree that there is at least some chance this is indeed, or could easily become, a crisis.

This evaluation process is termed: **crisis recognition**. First you must ask yourself, "Is this event a crisis?" If you make the assumption that you are always either in a crisis or a pre-crisis situation, then you can regard almost any event as a potential crisis, if not yet an actual full blown crisis. Once you have decided that a given event is in fact a real crisis you need to classify that event as either a **major** or **minor crisis**.

Won't you drive yourself crazy maintaining this level of paranoia every waking minute? The potential certainly exists. In fact this could even become a crisis.

Refer back to the emergency room model for a moment. Every patient who walks through the door of the ER is a potential crisis by definition. In fact it is fairly likely that the physician can and should intervene in the course of whatever process is occurring in almost every case, in order to have a positive effect at the critical turning point. This intervention may be dramatic and complex as in the cardiac arrest case presented in Chapter 1, or it may be as mundane and simple as splinting a sprained ankle.

Do emergency physicians get stressed out dealing with a series of non-stop crises every day? No. Not really - for several reasons. First, since every patient is a crisis of some sort, emergency physicians become accustomed to dealing with crisis. "Everyday Crisis Management" simply becomes part of their job description. Second, emergency physicians receive extensive preparation, training and practice in handling crisis, both major and minor. So when a crisis occurs they are adept at recognizing it and both knowledgeable and skilled in exactly what to do.

The lesson of this construct and you must come to accept it, is that crisis occurs all around you continually. If you practice dealing with these multiple minor crises on a regular basis, utilizing the tools of crisis management, you also will become more confident and adept at handling them. You will then be better able to prepare for a major crisis, recognize it and manage it successfully.

Every crisis exhibits certain common factors. Unexpected change, often sudden in nature, is a key characteristic of crisis. Conflict, or the potential for conflict, may be present. Decision on the part of an individual or group is usually necessary. Significant consequences, both positive and negative may hinge on the results of decision-making. Uncertainty of the outcome is almost always present. Lastly, there may be fear.

CHANGE
CONFLICT
DECISION
CONSEQUENCES
UNCERTAINTY
FEAR

Be alert for these signs and symptoms of crisis. Above all use your sense of intuition or gut feeling. When you recognize them make a mental note, "This may be the beginning of a crisis". You need to be aware of physical, environmental, societal, situational and organizational signs of change. Be alert to your surroundings and environment. Use all your senses: sight, hearing, touch and even smell.

Let's think back to previous examples. In the case

of the elevator gunman, crisis was obvious. All the elements noted above could be said to be present. But what if the other person in the elevator was a teen-age boy with a realistic looking toy pistol? Might it be harder to tell? Perhaps. It depends on your senses and judgment. How do you develop the ability to sense and judge a crisis? You develop it through practice. You must practice every day.

A young musician, late for his audition, hurried down a New York City street carrying a violin case. He stopped an elderly gentleman to ask directions.

"How do you get to Carnegie Hall?" he asked. The old man pondered the question for a moment and then replied, "Practice, practice, practice."

EXERCISE

Write the characteristics of crisis listed immediately above on a 3X5 card (or in your hand-held computer) and put it in your purse or wallet. When a situation occurs, any situation, pull out the card and read it. Is this a crisis? Could it become one? For the purposes of this exercise it is perfectly appropriate to term even a relatively minor incident a crisis. It is a minor crisis. Apply the label liberally. You are learning the skill of crisis recognition at this point.

Once an event is recognized as a crisis the next step is to classify it as a major crisis or a minor crisis. What are the potential outcomes or consequences of this event? Are the potential consequences serious? In the emergency room I ask myself, "Is anybody going to die?" If the answer is yes, there are serious consequences, then this is a **major crisis**. If not, it is a **minor** one. Continue to practice this skill of **crisis recognition**. Shortly you will learn the skill of crisis management.

The advantages of this schema of classification are twofold. First it allows you to put the crisis in perspective. Most crisis situations will be minor. This is good. You can more comfortably practice your crisis management skills secure in the knowledge that, since this is only a minor crisis, the cost of failure will not be unacceptably high. By managing minor crises successfully and learning from your mistakes along the way, you will be much more confident and skillful in the management of a major crisis.

Second, it forces you to face reality when a major crisis does occur. You have just classified this event as a **major crisis**. It is now incumbent upon you to pull out all the stops, give this crisis your undivided attention and manage it intensively.

Before you dismiss this exercise as silly or trite, let me say that this is exactly how emergency physicians approach each patient. Within minutes or even seconds, based on our observations and evaluation, we have formed an opinion that the patient is either major or minor. This allows us to prioritize care and adopt the appropriate sense of urgency in the approach to each patient. Our opinion may change in light of new information or subsequent developments, but it is constantly being made and acted upon. You could do a lot worse, in terms of learning crisis management, than to adopt the methods of those of us who manage crisis, quite literally, every day.

The 3X5 card is a mnemonic device I personally find very effective. I highly recommend it for this or any similar project. If you use it consistently over a period of time you will develop the ability to "read" the card without pulling it out. It can be tremendously reassuring, especially in a crisis situation when you tend to have memory lapses. The key to this device, as with many teaching tools, is to keep it simple.

EXERCISE

List three examples of potential societal crisis.

List three examples of potential business or personal crisis.

Would you recognize them as a crisis should they occur?

What crisis specific signs and symptoms might help in identification?

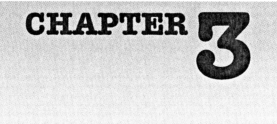

CRISIS PREDICTION

You have learned the basics of how to recognize a crisis and you are practicing daily with your 3X5 card. Wouldn't it be nice to be able to **predict** a crisis before it occurs? This is really quite simple. **A crisis will occur.** You can't always tell when, where, how, or what kind of crisis. But you can forecast with absolute certainty that at some point in the future a crisis will occur. It will happen to me. It will happen to you. It will happen to society. You know this because it has been this way throughout recorded history.

One of the earliest examples of crisis prediction is recorded in the Bible, in the Book of Genesis, chapter 41. In this story Joseph is brought before the Pharaoh of Egypt because of his reputation for accurate prediction of crisis, ostensibly through the interpretation of dreams. Joseph predicts a crisis, in the form of a famine. Luckily, Joseph predicts, there is some lead-time to prepare for this crisis. Joseph advises that Pharaoh appoint a crisis manager, who can supervise preparatory efforts and store up grain for this famine which is due to occur in 7 years. Naturally, Pharaoh appoints Joseph as crisis manager since he appears to be an expert in this sort of endeavor. This by the way resolves a personal crisis for Joseph. It gets him out of prison and into a very responsible government position. Joseph was a very good crisis manager.

Perhaps crisis prediction is not so hard after all. Crisis is inevitable. This is why crisis prediction is such a good business. But what's the value in predicting the inevitable? The value, as illustrated in the Bible story and the other examples of crisis we will discuss, is that a predicted crisis can be prepared for specifically or perhaps even prevented. There are also certain generic tools that have broad applicability to most, if not all, crisis situations. If you learn and practice these you will be much better equipped to deal with any type of crisis.

But how do you predict a specific crisis? At first blush this seems somewhat more difficult. How did Joseph predict the famine? How does an emergency physician predict a heart attack? How does one predict whether he or she will be held up in an elevator at gunpoint? This is not quite as easy, but again, easier than it seems at first. For example, on any given day it is highly likely that a patient with a heart attack will come to a big city emergency room. It is a virtual certainty that several patients will present with the complaint of chest pain and have to be evaluated for a possible heart attack. Given this level of daily probability, doesn't it make sense that emergency physicians should be highly prepared and trained to deal with heart attacks?

How do you predict an event like the elevator holdup? Well, it might be somewhat of a challenge to predict the timing of such an event. However, it is fair to say that if you live in a high crime neighborhood long enough the odds of some similar scenario occurring are pretty good. Is the probability high enough to warrant preparation and training? Would you classify this as a major or a minor crisis? Is anybody going to die? Enough said.

Wait a minute. Hold on. How did Joseph know that the famine would occur in seven years, or even that it would occur at all? Was he divinely inspired? Perhaps. Or perhaps he was simply an astute observer of nature and human nature as well. Joseph, you'll remember had previous occupational experience as a shepherd. So he probably had some insight into natural cycles. If the famine had occurred after only six years do you think Pharaoh would have been upset? If it had taken more than 8 or 9 years Joseph might have lost some credibility, but in the meantime he had a chance to prove his abilities and would be a lot better off than he was in prison. What was the downside of having an emergency supply of grain anyway?

Do we as individuals or as a society benefit from crisis prediction? You could sit around all day long in meetings speculating on which major or minor crisis might occur. Limitless resources could be expended in the name of crisis preparation and training. How many people who grew up in the 50's remember the government's advice on building back yard fall-out shelters in case of nuclear attack? Do any of you remember the swine flu non-epidemic of 1976? What about the Y2K computer non-crisis? Were these efforts to prepare for a crisis that never materialized bad or wasteful?

The key to addressing this question is **judgment**. You must individually and collectively decide which potential crisis merits your time, attention and resources. This isn't easy, given the multitude of potential crisis scenarios, but let's offer some guidelines. A major crisis that occurs with high frequency, such as a hurricane on the Atlantic seaboard, certainly deserves your attention in regard to planning and preparation. Less frequent but life threatening situations, such as a fire at home or at work, should be considered due to the possibility of serious consequences. Potential crisis situations of lesser severity and likelihood need to be evaluated on a case by case basis. It would be both impossible and exhausting to try to formulate specific plans for every crisis imaginable. However you can and certainly should, have a generic plan to deal with an unpredicted crisis.

Emergency physicians prepare and train specifically based on the crisis situations which have occurred commonly in the past. We know from previous experience that we will see heart attacks, gunshot wounds, sore throats and low back pain again and again. There is essentially a checklist of emergencies, major and minor, which occur on a quite regular, predictable basis. We then train generically to cover all the "zebras" (as in, "If you're hearing hoof-beats in Texas don't think of zebras."), which occur more rarely.

How do you recognize the **pre-crisis** phase? This is even easier. If you are not in **crisis** you must be in **pre-crisis**, since you now know for certain that **a crisis will occur.**

Review the principles of **crisis prediction**:

A CRISIS WILL OCCUR

You always are either in **CRISIS** or **PRE-CRISIS**.

EXERCISE

Refer back to the crisis situations you listed at the end of chapter 2. Are any of them predictable? Assign a probability to each one based on your experience, reference to appropriate resource material or consultation with an expert.

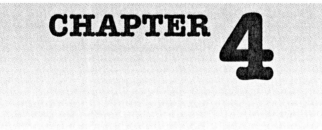

CRISIS PREVENTION

Now that you have learned how to predict a crisis let's see if you can use this information to **prevent** one. In the pursuit of preventing a crisis it is useful to introduce certain principles of prevention:

RISK FACTORS
DECREASE RISK AND UNCERTAINTY
MITIGATE INJURY
JUDGMENT

First let's examine the concept of **risk factors**. A risk factor is an underlying fact or reality that tends to increase the statistical incidence of a given event. You need to understand that certain risk factors predispose to any given crisis. In order to change the odds in your favor and try to prevent the crisis from occurring you must modify one or more of these risk factors.

For our first example let's return to the holdup in the elevator. If you accept the predictability of this event what steps could you have taken to prevent it? What are the risk factors for becoming the victim of an armed robbery? One would be living or working in a high crime neighborhood. A second might be having an appearance of affluence. Another might be appearing to be a relatively easy target. The easy availability of firearms in the neighborhood may play a role. What interventions could be postulated to decrease risk and uncertainty? How about moving and arranging to live and work in a low crime area? You could certainly avoid the obvious appearance of affluence, by not wearing expensive jewelry, driving a flashy car, or showing large amounts of cash in a store or on the street. Adopting a confident manner and appearance, hiring a body guard, organizing a neighborhood watch group, or effective gun control might also help alter the odds in favor of prevention.

How about **mitigating injury**? Wearing a bulletproof vest might make some sense. Is this practical? They are relatively heavy, hot during the summer and can cost $1000. While this is probably not a practical strategy for the average citizen, it may well be reasonable for a police officer. Here is an example of the need to exercise **judgment** in adopting prudent and feasible strategies to both **decrease risk and uncertainty** and **mitigate injury**.

For our next example return to the emergency room. Heart attack prevention is well documented in the medical literature. Major risk factors include hypertension, diabetes, high cholesterol, cigarette smoking and positive family history. While you can't control who your ancestors are, the remaining factors are to a large degree amenable to change. If the patient in Chapter 1 had come to see a physician some years prior to his event, been persuaded to quit smoking and probably placed on cholesterol lowering therapy, it is likely his heart attack could have been avoided, or at least postponed until much later in life. Is it worth modifying these **risk factors** at the cost of adopting a lifestyle you may find burdensome or unpleasant? This becomes an individual decision. Some might say, "I'd rather smoke, eat what I want and lead a shorter life than be constantly bothered by dietary restriction and having to give up my favorite habit." This again is a matter of **judgment**. My point is it should be a conscious decision in the face of full knowledge of the probability and risks, not one made by default.

In terms of **mitigating injury** our patient's **judgment** in finally going to the emergency room for his chest pain undoubtedly saved his life.

Okay, you're thinking, perhaps some events are preventable, but some things just happen. What about accidents? An accident is defined as, "Anything occurring unexpectedly, or without known or assignable cause." This seems at odds with our understanding of the predictability of crisis. For this reason scientists in the automotive field prefer to use the term collision rather than accident.

Motor vehicle collisions provide an excellent example of **crisis prevention** in practice. On average, one in 70 people in the US will die in a motor vehicle collision. Motor vehicle trauma is the leading cause of death between the ages of 1 and 40. One in three Americans will sustain a disabling injury in a crash at some time during their life. The average car will be involved in at least 1 collision at some point during its useful life. The probability of any individual driver being involved in a collision at some point is virtually 100%. So much for predictability. To paraphrase myself, "A collision will occur."

Does it make sense for everyone who drives or rides in a vehicle to address the issue of motor vehicle injury prevention on a personal level? I think so, don't you? How can we do it? Luckily for all of us, the science has been done well in this particular field. James Haddon MD, one of the pioneers of motor vehicle collision research, felt that there were three **risk factors** involved in any collision which related to the collision itself and resulting injuries: Human, vehicle, environment.

An example might be:

Human	Inexperienced driver, no seatbelt
Vehicle	Small car with poor safety design
Environment	Ice on the road

Any one factor alone, or even two of these factors together, might still leave us with some margin of safety. When all three combine you have a potentially very dangerous situation. What could be done to **decrease risk and uncertainty** and/or **mitigate injury**? You could certainly get some driver training for your inexperienced operator and persuade him to use a seatbelt. Less obvious is the idea of purchasing a safer vehicle in the first place. Every year the Insurance Institute for Highway Safety rates cars and trucks based on actual fatality, injury and cost outcomes from real life crashes. This information is available to the general public on their web-site (www.carsafety.com) and by mail (see the resources section). All other things being equal, why not drive the safest vehicle you can afford? Finally, isn't it prudent to avoid driving on icy days?

As a long time advocate I can tell you that prevention as a strategy suffers from one major shortcoming. It lacks drama. You don't see the heart attack you prevented or the crime that's never committed. People uninjured in a motor vehicle crash often ascribe their avoidance of injury to "good luck" rather than good automotive design.

Statistically you can demonstrate that the overall incidence of heart attacks or crimes has been reduced. You may even prove cause and effect relating to your interventions. Nevertheless prevention is seen as mundane and boring by many. It lacks the dramatic appeal of acute events.

One incident I vividly recall that does illustrate the concept of prevention involved a single vehicle collision. The patient, a sprightly lady in her 70's named Louise Beauchamp*, was driving home alone from a family get-together late at night. Although she had not consumed any alcohol it had been a long day and she was tired. She fell asleep at the wheel. Her car drifted to the right, veered off the road and struck a rather large oak tree at a speed paramedics estimated to be about 40 miles per hour. It rolled over at least 3 times, possibly 4, based on its location relative to the tree and damage to the roof. Then the car caught fire and burned. After overhearing fragments of the radio report from the ambulance I assembled the trauma team, fully expecting a critically injured, horribly burned, patient.

Mrs. Beauchamp arrived in the emergency room sitting up on the stretcher, awake, alert and pleasantly protesting that she wasn't hurt very much. She had refused the cervical collar and backboard treatment customary in trauma cases. Further history from the paramedics revealed that they had found Mrs. Beauchamp sitting in the grass, some distance from her burning car. Although she doesn't remember the accident, she apparently unbuckled her seatbelt following the crash and stepped out of the car before it caught fire. After examining her several times the only injury I could find was a single broken rib. At her insistence she was released from the hospital that night and went home with her husband.

Per my request she later sent me a picture of her car. It was a large late model foreign-made sedan, one of the first to have a driver's side airbag as standard equipment. All the paint had been burned off and the front end was smashed in a deep V, but the passenger compartment was completely intact. The roof had not collapsed.

This case immediately brought back sad memories of another patient I had seen a few years before. She was a slim, attractive woman in her mid 20's who had been riding with her boyfriend in a pickup truck. He had a few drinks too many and the truck left the road, also hitting a tree. The impact speed was not terribly fast, because the pickup was said to be mostly intact. The driver sustained several rib fractures but was awake and yelling loudly. His passenger, tragically, was dead. She had been pronounced at the scene, but I was asked to take a look at her. My first impression was that she looked more asleep than dead. Her long blond hair, streaming next to her on the stretcher, was unstained by blood. There wasn't a mark on her face or any other part of her body. The only physical signs were the fixed and dilated pupils in her light blue eyes. A post-mortem spine x-ray revealed the cause of death. Her neck was broken through the third cervical vertebrae. She must have struck the header bar, just above the windshield. Her neck flexed backward and snapped, severing the spinal cord. After that she never took another breath.

Her seat belt had not been buckled. There was no airbag in the pickup truck, which also had a fairly rigid steel frame, unlike the more shock absorbent "crumple zones" now designed into passenger cars.

Is it possible that some of the "non-crisis" events mentioned previously were prevented in whole or in part because they were predicted? Did an increased state of alertness, careful attention to diplomacy and military preparedness decrease risk and uncertainty, averting nuclear catastrophe and ultimately lead to the ending of the cold war? Did widespread vaccination in 1976 prevent the repetition of a deadly 1918 influenza pandemic? Did the billions of dollars spent preparing to deal with potential ramifications of the year 2000 computer bug prevent technological disaster? Perhaps by managing risk and uncertainty some of these and innumerable other, potential crisis events were averted. Learn to appreciate the mundane and boring techniques of **prevention.**

EXERCISE

Briefly review the principles of prevention:

Understand **risk factors**.

Work continuously to **decrease risk and uncertainty**.

Use **judgment** regarding probability and severity.

Attempt to **mitigate injury**.

What real situations in your own life can you think of that might lend themselves to prevention? Return to your list of recognized and predicted crisis situations from the previous chapters. Choose one or several. How would you apply and implement the principles of crisis prevention?

Mrs. B's car. The popped up trunk shows the original pink paint before the car burned.

Deflated post-deployment airbag, from a different vehicle.

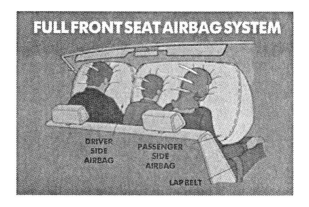

Prevention in practice: the way an airbag works.

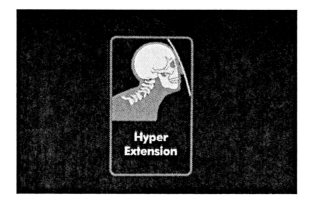

Mechanism of injury to the cervical spine, no airbag.

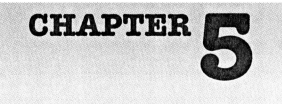

CHAPTER 5

PLANNING

In addition to trying our best to prevent crisis, it seems prudent to plan for the crisis we cannot prevent, as well as for the one we cannot even predict.

We will address the first category first. A predictable crisis, which is already the object of our efforts at prevention, likewise permits us to engage in planning, preparation and training. This type of crisis is a definable, discrete event, with a relatively high incidence, such as a heart attack or automobile collision.

In the heart attack model of course, it makes sense to intensively plan and prepare for heart attacks in the emergency room and cardiac intensive care unit. Likewise it makes sense to train cardiologists, emergency physicians, internists and family practitioners thoroughly in the state of the art treatment of heart attack. Further analysis however, reveals that most heart attacks actually occur outside the hospital. Since it is not feasible to provide advanced levels of care everywhere in the community, the solution chosen in this country was to train paramedics in the necessary emergency skills and send them out into the community to provide advanced care on the way to the hospital. In other parts of the world doctors actually ride in the ambulance and care for patients. The final link in this cardiac care chain of survival is the training of citizens in the community in basic skills of cardiopulmonary resuscitation (CPR). Most recently automatic external defibrillators (AEDs) are being placed strategically in public places, such as airports.

While you may intuitively grasp the value of planning for a predicted crisis, it may be difficult to understand the value of planning for an unpredictable crisis. It is even more difficult to understand how. The plain truth however, is that in many, perhaps even most instances, crisis is unpredicted, although not necessarily unpredictable. It behooves us therefore to develop and collect a number of "generic" crisis plans along with a general strategy of crisis management that will enable us to deal with the unpredicted crisis.

While **planning**, **preparation** and **training** are integrally related, we will separate them for the sake of clarity and deal with each in turn.

Before we can prepare or train we must have a **plan**. This can be as simple as an idea we have thought about for a few minutes or as complex as a document of many hundreds of pages formulated by a panel of world-renowned experts. How involved and formal a **crisis plan** needs to be depends on the crisis and the individual or organization it is designed for. For the purposes of learning crisis management it is important that you write down the plan, no matter how trivial or simple the problem.

A good **crisis plan** will contain the following basic elements:

> LEADERSHIP
> CHAIN OF COMMAND
> RESPONSIBILITY
> LOGISTICS
> COMMUNICATION
> CONTINGENCIES

Leadership is the ability to lead, guide, or exert authority. It can be critical in any crisis situation to have a prepared leader, who is familiar with the plan, in charge of executing it. Through the **chain of command** structure all others involved should understand whom they report to and likewise who reports to them. The **responsibility** of each individual involved must be explicit and be understood by that individual. **Logistics** involves that part of the plan dealing with the procurement and maintenance of necessary supplies and equipment. **Communication** refers to transferring information between the leader and other members of the team as well as interested or involved third parties. This includes communication of the components of the crisis plan itself. **Contingencies** consist of events which may not be addressed in the basic crisis plan, but which might possibly occur to upset the plan.

A good crisis plan will be as simple as possible, in accordance with the **kiss principle.** In its basic form: keep it simple, stupid. This is a practical application of Murphy's Law. The fewer steps, people, pieces of equipment and organizations involved, the less likely something will go wrong.

Useful tools of crisis planning include **algorithms**, **cookbooks** and **checklists**. An algorithm is basically a decision tree with branch points at each decision. If a certain fact is present we do A, if not we do B. It can be very simple and straightforward or complicated with many branches. Again, the simpler we can keep it the better it will work. The advantage of the algorithm is that it allows you to make the decision ahead of time, in light of the best research and knowledge and free from the pressure of an acute crisis situation. Perhaps you can even get a panel of experts to make the decision for you. It also allows you to provide for the most common contingencies. Then when crunch time comes and you're in a **major crisis** you refer to the appropriate algorithm and automatically make the right decision. Algorithms are used extensively in emergency medicine, especially in the treatment of complex cardiac problems. On the opposite page is an abbreviated example of the initial cardiac care algorithm.

Cookbooks are probably more familiar. Mix together ingredients A, B, C and D according to the directions. Bake in the oven for one hour and you have a cake. This sort of instruction sheet can be very handy in a crisis. Use it for infrequently performed procedures, or even more common ones that are critical. It may also be handy for new personnel who may be less familiar with even routine tasks. Keep it simple, one page if possible and available. Laminate it and attach it to the equipment or hang it on the wall.

In a similar vein, a checklist is a useful tool to be included in the plan. Any long sequence of events presents the possibility of failure if we are reliant on memory. If a checklist is available, however, the

ALGORTIHM FOR ADULT EMERGENCY CARDIAC CARE

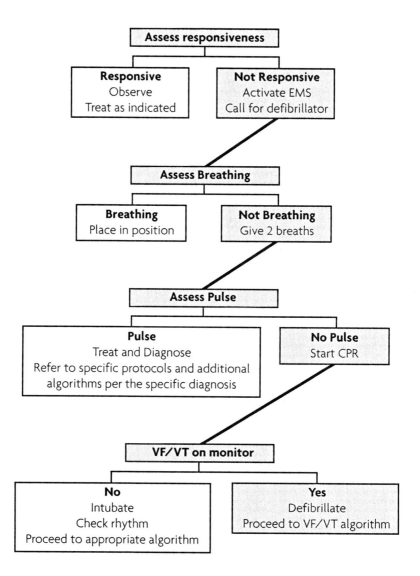

chance of omitting a critical step is greatly reduced. Remember, crisis management is all about reducing risk and uncertainty. A good example of a checklist is the preflight checklist used by pilots to ready an airplane for takeoff. By committing the long list of preflight tasks to paper the chance of error by omission is greatly reduced. Checklists can be attached to equipment, stuck to gearbags, kept on a wallet card, or laminated and hung on the wall.

PREFLIGHT CHECKLIST - CESSNA 172
FIRST
1. Fuel quantity: Check visually for desired level in both tanks.
2. Fuel filler caps: Check secure.
3. Windshield: Check.

CABIN
1. Pilot's operating handbook: Available in the airplane.
2. Control wheel lock: Remove.
3. Ignition switch: Off.
4. Master Switch: On.
5. Fuel quantity indicators: Check quantity.
6. Flaps: 10 degrees, check for proper extension.
7. Master switch: Off
8. Fuel selector valve: Both
9. LEFT WING...

This basic checklist goes on for another several pages and will not be reproduced here in its entirety, since the point is not to teach you to fly. I hope you are convinced, however, that a checklist is a useful tool to assure the completion of a critical series of steps, any one of which might easily be forgotten without it.

PLAN A AND PLAN B

What do you do when your initial plan (plan A) doesn't work? Sometimes a change in circumstances, unpredicted contingencies, malfunctioning equipment, or poor planning will result in the failure of our plan. In this case it is handy to be able to trot out plan B. Plan B need not necessarily be as complete or well rehearsed as plan A. After all you feel that plan A is a good plan and should work the vast majority of times. But in the rare instance where plan A is not workable it sure is comforting to have plan B in reserve. The only alternative to having plan B is "winging it". This is not a particularly attractive alternative since most people cannot depend on doing the right thing automatically in time of crisis without previous planning, preparation and training.

Do you need plans C, D and E in case plan B doesn't work? You probably do not. You are reaching the point of diminishing returns. Most contingencies should be considered and addressed in plans A and B. By the time you get to plan C you are beyond what most of us can remember anyway.

How do you know when to give up on plan A and go to plan B? The rule of thumb, as stated by Dr. Pierce Gardner, one of my medical school professors, is simple, "If something is working keep doing it. If it's not working, stop doing it and do something else." The decision to abandon plan A and go to plan B must be based on your best **judgment** at the time.

A sobering episode illustrating the above points occurred to Delia Pachinko* on the Wolf River in northern Wisconsin. Delia was kayaking one cold spring day in 1978 with friends from college. The river was high and the rapids nothing short of ferocious. Gray-green water rolled over submerged boulders in gigantic thundering arcs and formed huge standing waves just down-river. The water temperature was a killing 45 degrees fahrenheit.

Delia felt a little nervous, but she was an expert kayaker and trained scuba diver. She double-checked all of her safety equipment. It included a full wet suit, helmet and life jacket. The people she was with were all experienced kayakers. She thought she would be able to handle the river. The group put in and headed down-river.

The first set of rapids was a warm-up. Nothing too challenging or dangerous. The feeling of sliding through the churning cataracts unscathed was exhilarating. After a brief stretch of quiet water the group headed for the next rapids. A dull roar became audible and increased exponentially as they approached. A line stretched in front of them where the river seemed to end, as if it just dropped away. Flecks of foam jumped up above the line from time to time like baitfish trying to escape a blitzing school of predatory bluefish.

The lead paddler swung to the left side of the river and his kayak tipped down sharply, indicating

Powering through a hydraulic in a white-water raft.

the favored entry point into the rapids. Delia was close behind him, second in line. She darted over the fall line and down the steep slope of the rapids. Her kayak swept over a great green hump of river and then stopped dead as the bow bit into the standing wave below it. Suddenly all she saw was foam. Sucked out of the kayak, like a bug going down a drain, she was totally enveloped in cold dark water.

Kicking for the surface she swam steadily upward. She had become disoriented in the dunking, but she followed air bubbles toward the surface, just as she had been taught in her scuba training. Wearing a full wet suit and life vest, she was extremely buoyant. She should bob up like a cork. Yet, after swimming vigorously for over 20 seconds she hadn't broken the surface. The river wasn't that deep. Something was wrong!

Only seconds were left before hypoxia would rob her of consciousness. She had to do something different. She had to adopt a different plan. Instantly Delia changed direction 180 degrees and swam the opposite way. Immediately she collided with the bottom of the river, was swept downstream and then popped effortlessly to the surface.

Delia had been "sucked down a hydraulic", a downward flowing column of water in the middle of the river caused by water cascading over a huge rock. While her plan A would ordinarily have worked, she had been in the one circumstance where it would not. It was the equivalent of trying to swim up a waterfall. Through rapid assessment of her situation Delia was able to abandon plan A, which wasn't working and adopt plan B which did.

I heard a strikingly similar story told one day by a man who had gone on a guided white-water rafting expedition. He was thrown from the raft in mid-rapids and likewise sucked down a hydraulic. After fighting frantically for as long as the air in his lungs permitted, he lost consciousness. Luckily for him he eventually bobbed to the surface, was plucked from the river by a guide and resuscitated.

GENERIC PLANS

As we mentioned earlier in this chapter, sometimes you come up against a crisis for which you have no specific plan. In these cases you can often adopt a generic plan based on the elements of the specific crisis plan: **Leadership, chain of command, responsibilities, logistics, communication and contingencies**. Often, in an organization for example, most of these elements will already be in place.

The emergency room, as a case in point, is fundamentally organized around the framework of a generic crisis plan. All the basic elements have been addressed ahead of time in a way that allows their application to multiple different crisis situations. While emergency physicians never know from one moment to the next the specific type or magnitude of crisis that will come through the door, we achieve the flexibility to deal competently with a large number and variety of crisis situations. We are virtually prepared to deal with anything.

WINGING IT/PLANNING IN 30 SECONDS FLAT

On occasion, hopefully rare, you will find yourself without a plan. This may occur due to a failure to predict a crisis, failure to plan for a predicted crisis, or failure of the plan to work as expected. Notice the repetition of the word failure. I don't like this word.

I don't like the implications of winging it. If you have already experienced multiple failures what are your chances of success without a well thought out plan? Not nearly as good. Do not make a habit of reliance on winging it as a primary strategy. It is a recipe for disaster.

Before resorting to the winging it strategy briefly review. Are you sure you don't have a plan for this eventuality? Could you perhaps adapt another plan or use a generic plan? If the answer is definitely not, you have to resort to "winging it", or rapidly formulating a plan. Sometimes a quickly conceived plan may work passably well. It is almost always better than no plan at all.

There are two main alternatives to rapidly formulating a plan or "winging it". These consist of either action without a plan, otherwise known as the trial and error method, or no action at all. The trial and error method is used extensively by lower forms of life: insects, worms and other invertebrate organisms. Through many generations of massive reproduction they evolve adaptive instinctual behaviors. This is not a good strategy for humans. We can't afford the time or attendant loss of life.

The no action strategy is likewise fraught with danger. You are letting someone else, or in many cases no one at all, decide the outcome of an event. You have in essence given up. You have no chance of tilting the odds in your favor.

So if you find yourself in a crisis situation without a plan, you may have to resort to "winging it" and rapidly formulate the best one possible under the circumstances. But please understand that this is an example of the least preferred method of managing a crisis, not a first alternative. Winging it is strictly for an unexpected crisis with no specific or generic plan.

Emergency physicians appear to be particularly adept at "winging it" when the unexpected happens. This is, to a very large degree, an illusion. What we in fact are really doing is dusting off and rolling out a generic or specific plan stored in our memory banks for this particular or some similar crisis. It is amazing how many times a plan drawn up for one crisis is adaptable for use in another. When this is not possible emergency physicians draw upon problem solving skills and previous training to rapidly formulate a plan. We perform a rapid assessment of the situation, decide upon a reasonable course and then act boldly and decisively to implement the plan. Since we have lots of practice in rapidly solving acute life threatening problems, "problem solving in 30 seconds or less" becomes a natural corollary of "everyday crisis management."

An interesting example of the technique of winging it (and also an example of a positive crisis) is a story told to me by Les Waal, an avid fisherman. Les was surf casting off a beach on Massachusetts Bay one summer day when he hooked into something unusually large.

"I knew it was a really big fish, because it hit the bait hard and then just kept going."

The heavy test line screamed off the reel.

"It wasn't long before it had taken all of my line."

This was the major crisis of Les's fishing career. The fish on his line was undoubtedly the biggest he had ever hooked. It had taken all his line and was still pulling ferociously. If he dug in and stood his ground on the beach the line would break. He couldn't reel the fish in while it continued to run. He could cut the line to save his surf casting pole, but then he would lose the fish.

Les began wading out into the surf, lured on inexorably by the fish. Wading farther and farther, soon he was waist deep. Then the gentle slope of the beach suddenly dropped off and he was swimming. The fish was towing him out into the Atlantic. Les refused to give up. He searched his mind rapidly for a plan. Visions of Santiago, Ernest Hemingway's fisherman character in "The Old Man and the Sea", flashed through his head. He needed a boat! Armed with his newly formulated plan Les started yelling as loud as he could, still keeping his rod tip up to prevent the fish from breaking the line. A nearby fisherman in a small flat-bottomed skiff heard the commotion and motored over to help. He managed to haul Les into the boat and together they continued to fight the fish. Eventually they were able to bring the huge tuna alongside and get it to shore. It weighed in at more than 600 pounds.

Another good example of winging it involves the rapid integration of previous knowledge and training to formulate a workable plan in "30 seconds or less". John Peltin MD* had a keen interest in the science of collisions and trauma based on the cases he saw on a regular basis in the ER. He read extensively and had a good understanding of the relationships between forces applied and injuries sustained. One winter day he had an opportunity to personally test the concepts he had learned.

Following a series of heavy snowfalls the weather had warmed resulting in a sudden thaw. While standing outside admiring the winter wonderland in his front yard Peltin glanced up at the roof of his house. A heavy blanket of snow covered the roof and curled down over the edges. Water was beginning to drip down stalactite-like icicles hanging from the rain gutters. His short-lived reverie was interrupted by sudden fear. Ice dams in the gutters could result in water damage inside the house if they weren't cleared.

Anxious to inspect the gutters and try to clear any ice dams, he pulled the aluminum extension ladder out of his garage. He dug the feet of the ladder deeply and evenly into the snow to prevent it from slipping and climbed to the level of the roof edge to inspect the gutters. In some places the gutters were filled with snow and could be dug out by hand. In others they were filled with a solid block of ice. His anxiety growing, he approached the roofline in front of the garage.

The driveway in front of the garage was cleared of snow but still wet. It had been salted to prevent it from icing over. As he set up the ladder he realized that without any snow cover there would be no way to anchor the bottom of the ladder. He had no assistant to "foot" the ladder. For a moment he hesitated. He had seen too many falls from ladders.

He rested the ladder against the edge of the roofline and then extended it up to the roof of the bedroom above the garage. It seemed steady. With three points of contact it should be all right. He climbed to the level of the garage roof and inspected the gutter. It was clogged with ice. Water in the garage wouldn't be the worst problem. What about the roof of the bedroom above the garage? Cautiously he proceeded up the ladder toward the bedroom roofline.

As his weight shifted to the upper part of the ladder the edge of the garage roof began to act as a fulcrum, like a seesaw, taking weight and resistance away from the feet of the ladder. Suddenly the ladder started slipping. Peltin realized he was going down to the pavement. Was he better off to jump or stay on the ladder?

Luckily the speed of thought is even more rapid than acceleration due to gravity. Peltin says he "instinctively" knew what to do based on his knowledge and experience, but for the benefit of readers the reasoning is as follows: G (gravitational) forces involved in collisions are a function of the velocity (speed) at the time of collision and are modified by the surface area involved in the impact and the rate of deceleration at impact. In other words, the faster you fall, the faster you stop falling and the more the forces are concentrated onto a single point, the worse the injuries sustained. This translates into the common sense notion that any fall from a high place to a hard surface is bad.

Peltin knew that if he jumped from the ladder he would travel the 16 feet straight down to the pavement in exactly one second. He would hit the driveway traveling at exactly 32 feet per second (20 MPH) and would probably land on one or both feet in a nearly vertical orientation, before collapsing further to the asphalt. He would most likely break one or both ankles, perhaps a foot and risked significant injuries to his hips and spine. If he remained on the upper surface of the ladder, however, it would take significantly longer to reach the ground, perhaps more than 2 seconds. His acceleration (and therefore his final velocity) would be much slower as the ladder slid down the roof as opposed to a 16-foot "free fall" drop. Furthermore his surface contact area at impact would be much greater, since it would be spread out along his entire body, horizontally, on the ladder.

Did all this flash through his mind in an instant? In any case, in less than the blink of an eye, he made the decision to ride the ladder down. Spread-eagled along the upper surface of the ladder, he clattered down the roof and followed the ladder to the asphalt in a loud aluminum crash. Momentarily stunned, he lay on top of the ladder. The wind had been knocked out of his lungs.

The wonderful thing about science is its usefulness in predicting events based upon the laws of nature. As Peltin lay on the ladder he began to consciously inventory his body parts. He had no pain in his head or neck. He was a little out of breath, but had no pain in his chest, abdomen or pelvis. No pain in the arms or legs. Cautiously he got off the ladder and stood up. He couldn't believe he was uninjured from a 16-foot fall to the pavement. As he climbed the steps to go back inside a sudden pain in his knee announced the only injury. It turned out to be a hairline crack in the patella (kneecap) which had been pressed against one of the ladder rungs when he landed. It healed without a cast or surgery.

Several months later Dr. Peltin saw a patient in the emergency room who fell a similar distance from the second floor roofline. He landed in a vertical orientation and impacted the ground feet first, then on his buttocks. He sustained a compression fracture of his 12th thoracic vertebrae which ruptured in a bursting fashion and cut the spinal cord. The man was rendered paraplegic from the injury, permanently paralyzed from the waist down.

ORGANIZATIONAL CRISIS PLANNING

Crisis planning in a business or organizational setting is by its very nature more complex and difficult than individual crisis planning. Large numbers of people are usually involved. It is crucial to insure their acceptance and participation in the plan.

The first step is to establish the authority to create such a plan. The commitment of the leader, be his title CEO, owner, director or something of this sort, is critical. The next step is to assemble a planning team. Not only will this allow you the benefit of other people's knowledge and experience, but it will also result in a sense of "ownership" which is important to adoption and widespread acceptance of the plan. An additional benefit will be the ability to delegate and spread out the workload. The team should include members, or at a minimum significant input, from upper management and all operational areas involved in the plan. In large organizations or formal settings a plan document is appropriate, with a mission statement, budget, list of members and delineation of responsibilities.

The next step is to gather information regarding possible hazards and emergencies. These may include problems specific to the organization, such as hazardous materials used in a manufacturing process, as well as generic issues such as fire, earthquake, or severe storms. Analyze the vulnerabilities of the organization to potential major hazards.

The following list is a good starting point:

Historical: What events have occurred in the past at this facility or similar facilities of this type?
Fire
Power failure
Terrorism or sabotage

Geographic: List events that may occur due to the specific location.
Flood
Earthquake
Radioactive accidents
Train, plane, or automobile crashes

Technological: Think about the technology you depend on and the consequences of its failure.
Explosion
Computer failure
Telecommunication failure
Hazardous materials incident
Heating or cooling system failure
Emergency alarm failure

Human error: Consider events that could occur due to lack of training, carelessness, substance abuse, or fatigue.
Vehicle crashes
Safety system failures
Diplomatic incidents
Hazardous material spills

Physical plant factors: How might the design or construction of the actual physical facility contribute to the risk of a crisis?
Evacuation considerations
Strength and details of construction
Hazardous materials storage
Lighting
Location of equipment

Regulatory factors: Could action by regulatory agencies cause a crisis?
Prohibited access to a facility
Restrictions on details of operation

Once you have listed all possible factors assign a probability to each one. This is only your best guess, but it may help you to know where you want to focus your resources in drawing up the plan. Realistically assess the potential consequences of each eventuality. Is there a possibility of death or injury? What would be the financial costs? What would be the costs due to interrupted or lost business?

Next review the current capabilities for dealing with each of these problems. What are you already prepared to do? What else needs to be done?

Obtain information and outside expertise as necessary from organizations such as utility companies, police, fire departments, government agencies and medical resources. Consult with other organizations similar to your own that may have already formulated solutions they may be willing to share.

Now you must develop a plan. The plan should include the following elements:

- EXECUTIVE SUMMARY
  The executive summary provides a brief overview of the plan. It should state the purpose of the plan, outline emergency policies and procedures, set forth the authority and responsibilities of key personnel, designate a central command center and list the major perceived types of emergencies which may occur.
- MANAGEMENT SECTION
  This is the "guts " of the plan. Be sure to address each of the major basic elements of a crisis plan:
- LEADERSHIP
- CHAIN OF COMMAND
- RESPONSIBILITY
- LOGISTICS
- COMMUNICATION
- CONTINGENCIES

Consider the utility of algorithms, checklists, diagrams and cookbooks. Make up an emergency telephone call list. Include these items in the plan and make laminated copies for posting where appropriate. Think about relevant details including: protection of employees, customers and equipment, evacuation procedures, shutting down operations and protecting vital records.

Obtain and include necessary documents such as building plans with the location of fire hydrants, utility shutoffs, fire extinguishers, exits, stairways, evacuation routes. Note the location of hazardous materials and valuable documents, equipment and materials.

List resources that may be necessary or useful in an emergency. Make sure they are accessible and that their location is noted in the plan. This may include other organizations such as police, fire, ambulance, or even neighboring businesses which may have agreed to provide support.

Once you have written the plan solicit comments from all segments of the organization. You need to be sure there is nothing major being overlooked. This will also help obtain a sense of ownership and commitment on the part of the entire enterprise.

After the plan has been written the hard work begins. It is not sufficient to have a neatly typed "disaster plan" filed away in some dusty drawer. The plan must be distributed throughout the organization and read. Then significant **preparation** and **training** must take place to assure that the plan can actually be **implemented** when the time comes.

EXERCISE

Write a **crisis plan** for your business, organization or family. Write a simple plan first. What would you and your family do if a fire occurred at home? List the elements of your plan: **Leadership, communication, logistics, responsibility** and **training.** What about contingencies: a fire at night, a gas explosion? Once you've developed the plan **communicate.** Discuss it with your family. Then **train** according to the plan. Prepare appropriate **logistical** equipment, such as a fire extinguisher, cell phone, rope ladder, etc.

Now draw up an organizational or business **crisis plan**. A fire occurs at your office. This is more complex. Your initial focus is of course on the safety of personnel, but what about the "life" of your organization? What happens if computers are burned or waterlogged?

Do you back up and store the computer files off site daily? From where will you resume operations if the office is a total loss? Where will the financial resources come from to weather such a crisis?

Ask lots of "what if " questions and formulate answers. Make up an **algorithm** and a **checklist**. Discuss the plan with your team at the organization. To function properly it must be their plan as well. They must "own" it, believe in it and train for it.

Resources to help write a business or personal crisis plan (and even some simple preprinted plans) are available from the Federal Emergency Management Agency (FEMA). Refer to the resources section at the end of the book.

CHAPTER 6

PREPARATION AND TRAINING

"Semper paratus" is the motto of the United States Marine Corps. It is Latin for, "Always prepared". Boy Scouts likewise adopt the motto, "Be prepared." What are all these people preparing for? The answer is - for whatever might happen. They are preparing mentally and physically, specifically and generically. They spend many long hours planning, preparing and training, so that they are ready when the time comes to act.

How does one prepare for a crisis and how is preparing different from planning? The first step is to have a plan. Once we have planned what to do we need to both prepare and train. Preparation involves both mental and physical components. Mentally we need to rehearse the plan. Go over it in our mind's eye and visualize its execution. What will we do if various contingencies occur? Do we have the necessary skills to execute the plan? Has the plan been communicated to our team? Do we need training? Do we have the equipment and supplies necessary to carry out the plan? Does the equipment need periodic maintenance? Do all team members know how to operate it?

It may make sense to assemble necessary equipment in a gear bag or box. A good example of this is the "crash cart" in the hospital Emergency Department. This is a wheeled cart which contains all the necessary equipment and supplies to conduct a cardiac resuscitation. The cart needs to be checked and restocked periodically, depending on its frequency of use. Certain pieces of equipment, such as the defibrillator need to be tested daily and serviced periodically. A list of contents should be attached to any such "gear bag" so that completeness can be easily verified and missing items restocked.

Another element of preparation is to put the plan to a test. This is where the concept of a drill comes in. A drill gives your team the opportunity to go through a "dry run" of the plan without the pressure of serious consequences attendant to an actual crisis. It allows you to run through various contingencies and may prompt you to think of others that have been overlooked in the plan. It lets you test equipment and personnel under conditions as close to an actual crisis as can reasonably be simulated.

Preparation may also involve physical conditioning, as in the armed services, or education in technical areas by the whole team or certain team members.

The value of personal preparation is well illustrated by this story about Katherine Thoreau.* Katherine was a 56-year-old widow who lived alone after the death of her husband. Although she had been an insulin-requiring diabetic since her teen-age years, Katherine refused to regard this as a "chronic disease". She had simply incorporated the necessary changes into her daily routine. She led an active life, working as an editor of children's books and visiting her daughter and three grandchildren whenever she could.

Always athletic, Katherine looked and felt much younger than her age. She had recently begun running in marathons and other competitive events. Because of her diabetes she was concerned about the possibility of an insulin reaction occurring during competition. Her doctor had counseled her regarding the appropriate regimen of insulin and in getting sufficient calories and fluids both before and during a race. But when he suggested a medic alert bracelet she balked. Katherine thought she would feel stigmatized by a bracelet and didn't want to handle constant questions about her health. She thought of herself as an "insulin deficient marathoner" rather than a "diabetic". She finally decided to compromise and, when she bought a new car, signed up for the optional Onstar ® system, which included a medical information alert service called Global Med-Net®. This featured a medallion she could carry in her purse and a sticker affixed to her driver's license. Having done this, Katherine felt prepared.

Aside from marathon running and her grandchildren, Katherine's other major hobby was gardening. She maintained a sizable plot in the local community garden on the edge of town where she grew flowers and vegetables. Often she rose early in the morning to weed and water the garden, which was on her way to work

One summer morning Katherine started off on her usual Wednesday routine. The only thing out of the ordinary was a breakfast meeting at the office. She injected her insulin, grabbed a glass of orange juice on her way out to tide her over until breakfast and drove to the garden plot to do some weeding before work. The last thing Katherine remembers was pulling on her gardening gloves.

She was found by a passerby out walking his dog nearly an hour later, lying unconscious in the dirt. The man called 911 on his cell phone and paramedics responded to the scene within minutes. She was suffering from low blood sugar, also known as insulin shock. As time goes by the risk of permanent brain damage from lack of vital nutrients increases. It had already been almost an hour since she passed out. The paramedics looked in her wallet for identification and found the Global Med-Net ® sticker on her driver's license with an 800 number. As one man started an IV, his partner called Global Med-Net on his cellular phone and was informed that Katherine was diabetic. Once he knew the cause of her coma he was able to provide immediate, definitive treatment. Moments after he injected an ampule of IV Dextrose (sugar) Katherine was sitting up and asking what had happened. She was then transported to the hospital where the doctor ordered her breakfast.

Katherine had prepared for a crisis. Her preparation had saved precious time when it counted most.

ORGANIZATIONAL PREPARATION

Refer back to the organizational crisis plan we have discussed in the previous chapter. What preparation needs to be made to assure your ability to implement the plan when the time comes? The first step is to distribute the plan and have people read it. They should at a minimum be familiar with the summary and the sections relevant to their individual area of responsibility.

The next step is to assemble the equipment necessary for logistical support, communications and other necessary elements of the plan. Test it to make sure that it works. There is nothing worse than a defibrillator that refuses to discharge during a real cardiac arrest, or a cell phone with dead batteries when you need to call 911. Practice using any equipment which is specialized, technical or unfamiliar. The time to learn how to use complex medical equipment, power tools, or communications equipment is in the **pre-crisis** phase, not during an emergency.

Then conduct a "table top" exercise. Assemble all involved parties in a room. Include at least one representative from each area or division. Present several mock crisis scenarios and verbally run through the workings of the plan. This is a good way to discover and iron out potential glitches as well as to familiarize people with the plan. Next each participant should go back to his team, explain what happened during the exercise and use this as an opportunity to acquaint his people with the plan. Drills may now be organized to rehearse the entire plan as well as any technical aspects. At this point a training schedule should be established for specific skill acquisition and periodic rehearsals of the entire plan. Personnel will change over time and memory will decay. Review the plan at regular, appropriate intervals.

Integrate the plan into the normal operations of your organization. Find opportunities to build awareness of the plan and to educate and train personnel. Conduct random tests to determine the readiness of the organization.

EXERCISE

Prepare for a predicted emergency by putting together a gearbox (such as a first aid kit) for your home or business. Consult knowledgeable sources regarding its contents. Put a renewal date on it, indicating when it should be restocked, checked and updated. Familiarize yourself and your team members with its contents, location and use.

EXERCISE 2

Conduct a "table top" rehearsal of the organizational crisis plan you have written based on the planning chapter.

TRAINING

What is training and how is it different from planning and preparing? Training can be defined as: to render skillful, proficient, or qualified by systematic instruction, drill, etc.

CPR (cardiopulmonary resuscitation) training is a good example. This is an intensively researched set of skills standardized by a professional sponsoring organization, the American Heart Association. CPR is taught by highly skilled, highly trained instructors, most of whom are medical professionals. This training is available to laymen as well as medical people and is rigorous and highly structured. It stresses mastery of certain basic physical and mental skills through repetitive practice, drill and assessment.

What other kinds of crisis related training can you think of? Fire drills, air raid drills, lifeguard training, first aid training. All these have a common purpose or goal - to achieve an automatic response along with tangible intellectual and physical skills. This automatic response or **training effect** can be invaluable in crisis situations

When we achieve a training effect specific pathways in the brain are set up to facilitate the efficient performance of a particular skill. An example of the training effect is what occurs when you learn to ride a bicycle. The first time you tried it, as a small child, it was difficult. You fell over. Eventually, through practice, a training effect took place and your brain became programmed for bicycle riding. Now, even years later, it is automatic behavior. You can get on the bicycle and ride, even if you haven't ridden in a long time. Scientific evidence for these brain pathways is sometimes seen in small strokes where patients can lose the ability to perform certain basic tasks, such as speaking, walking, or writing, which must then be retrained.

Training pays off in situations where we don't have the time to stop and think about the best course of action or where the best action may be obscure, require technical skills, or has been proven by previous experience. The time for training is in the pre-crisis period. There is often no time to train during a crisis.

A good example of training is the response to the cardiac arrest patient in chapter one. It went strictly according to an algorithm, which had been learned by rote and practiced over and over. The nurse performing cardiac massage had practiced this skill for many hours on the CPR manikin during training courses until it had become an automatic response. The placement of the endotracheal or breathing tube in the patient's airway is a complex physical skill perfected through study, individualized training and practice under supervision in many actual intubations. The respiratory therapist providing artificial ventilation had learned and practiced this skill repeatedly. The integrated functioning of the entire cardiac arrest team had been practiced by simulations during training courses and reinforced through periodic drills in the emergency room. It was Sophocles who said, "One must learn by doing the thing, for though you think you know it you have no certainty until you try."

Training can be utilized in a variety of crisis scenarios and should be designed to address specific issues that may apply to each individual's or organization's unique circumstances. An example of this might be training at a chemical plant relating to the proper handling of a hazardous materials leak. There are certain generic types of training, however, which can be generally recommended both to learn how to train and as useful personal skills. These include CPR of course, general first aid, basic self-defense, swimming and basic survival skills.

Physical conditioning is another good example of a generic crisis management skill that lends itself to training. In addition to helping us prepare for a crisis situation, it builds self-confidence and has been shown to elevate mood and improve one's health in general. Make sure to consult with your physician before undertaking any exercise regime, both in regard to its content and your readiness to undertake it.

Training played a key role in the 1989 crash landing of United Airlines flight 232 in Sioux City, Iowa. Sixty-seven minutes after takeoff, the DC-10 jet was cruising at 37,000 feet when a loud bang was heard and the airplane began to shudder. An explosion in the rear engine spewed out pieces of fan blade, which severed all three hydraulic fluid lines, completely disabling the hydraulic steering mechanism. As the pilot, Captain Alfred Haynes, ran through his engine shutdown checklist the flight engineer stated that all hydraulic pressure gauges indicated zero pressure. The big jet began a downward right turn and the first officer announced he could no longer control the airplane. At that point Captain Haynes took the controls and confirmed that the airplane was not responding. By reducing thrust in the number one engine he was able to level off. The flight crew deployed the auxiliary hydraulic pump, but they were unable to restore hydraulic power.

At 3:20 PM the flight crew radioed the air traffic control center in Minneapolis and requested directional vectors to the nearest airport. Rather than try to turn the aircraft the flight crew decided to continue on their established heading toward Sioux City, Iowa. The crew proceeded, as they had been **trained** to do, to prepare for an emergency landing. Excess jet fuel was dumped to minimize the **risk** of fire. Flight attendants prepared the passengers, making sure all seat belts were tightly fastened and instructing all passengers in the brace position for a crash landing. Babies and small children were padded with pillows to snug up their seat belts.

Captain Haynes, with the assistance of Captain Dennis Fitch who had been a passenger in first class, was able to control his direction by varying the thrust between the two remaining engines. Together they lined the plane up with runway 22 and began their approach into Sioux City.

Meanwhile, on the ground in Sioux City, the Federal Aviation Administration (FAA) control tower had notified the airport fire department at about 3:25 PM. Five fire and rescue vehicles were immediately dispatched. In addition the Sioux City Fire Department was notified and sent four more vehicles. Also notified were the Woodbury County Disaster and Emergency Services and county, state and local law enforcement personnel. The airport / county emergency services organization had conducted a full-scale disaster drill in 1987, two years prior to the incident. The airport fire and rescue teams had conducted a drill in June of 1989, just one month before the crash.

Utilizing the throttles of engines 1 and 3 as steering levers, the two captains descended along runway 22. The airplane touched down slightly to the left of the runway centerline at 4:00 PM. The right wing tip made ground contact first, followed by the right main landing gear. The airplane skidded to the right, rolled over, ignited and then cartwheeled. It crossed an adjacent runway and broke apart.

Firefighters and rescue personnel were lined up along the runway and ready as the plane landed. They immediately approached the burning wreckage and sprayed it with fire retardant foam to protect passengers exiting the wrecked plane. They assisted passengers into emergency vehicles and transported them to area hospitals.

The calm reaction of the pilot, plane crew and air traffic controller was attributable to their significant crisis related training. Coupled with that, the prompt, skillful, trained response of the Sioux City disaster crew, which had previously drilled for just such an emergency, saved the lives of 183 people even though the plane crash landed and burned. Captain Haynes had been able to maneuver the crippled plane to a crash landing at the airport where an immediate, trained response by the ground emergency crew was available. In a subsequent speech recounting the disaster, Captain Haynes urged both disaster crews and businesses to practice religiously what to do in an emergency.

DRILLS

One of my favorite teaching techniques in the emergency room is to run drills of various emergency scenarios. It is a wonderfully realistic exercise when conducted in the actual "code" or "trauma" room. It provides the opportunity to put students and resident physicians "on the spot" and forces them to make life or death decisions with only fear of embarrassment in front of their peers at stake, rather than someone's life. It also is an opportunity for the staff to review less frequently occurring emergencies with which they might not have much experience.

With this purpose in mind, I often conduct a pediatric cardiac arrest drill. Although pediatric cardiac arrests are not unusual in the neonatal intensive care unit or a pediatric emergency room, they are much less common in the general emergency room.

The drug dosages are all different from those used in an adult situation. The equipment utilized is somewhat different and the underlying problems are generally of a different nature. For these reasons periodic drills are a useful review. With this in mind, one particular day, I ran a pediatric arrest drill in the emergency room. We ran through several different scenarios, calculated medication dosages, reviewed potential problems of intravenous access and discussed the special techniques involved in intubation and securing of the pediatric airway. On the whole it was a very comprehensive review.

The very next day we received a six-year-old drowning victim in full cardiac arrest. The code proceeded flawlessly. The same staff members who had rehearsed this very event the day before were there again doing it for real. Unfortunately, we were unable to resuscitate the little boy. He had been underwater for too long. Although this case was tragic, we all felt good about the manner in which we ran the code and knew that we had done the very best job possible. It was important to all of us to know that we had performed in a highly competent manner—much more so in this tragic instance of failure than it would have been in a successful code.

The fact that we were well prepared and trained helped us to cope with defeat.

An example of the potential consequences of a lack of training was in evidence the day Jerry Samples* was brought to the emergency room following a seizure at work. Jerry had a history of epilepsy but had decided to "taper" his anti-seizure medication because he didn't think he still needed it. He was standing outside, in front of his office building, having a cigarette with some of his co-workers. Suddenly, Jerry cried out, fell to the ground and began shaking all over. His mouth was foaming like a rabid dog. The twitching of his arms and legs was uncontrollable and frightening to his friends, who had never seen an epileptic seizure before. Then, after a very long minute, the seizure was over and Jerry stopped breathing.

Now his co-workers were really terrified. A heavy-set middle aged woman took immediate action. She knelt over Jerry's limp body and began doing cardiac compressions, just like she had seen on TV. Never having had any training in CPR, or even basic first aid, she didn't stop to check for a pulse to see if the heart was still beating (which it was). She also didn't know that seizure patients often stop breathing and that respiration usually resumes spontaneously once the seizure has stopped. She didn't stop to reason out that cardiac compression without adequate ventilation (mouth to mouth breathing in this case) wouldn't do much good. She just doggedly continued to press on Jerry's chest until the ambulance arrived.

Luckily for Jerry he did not sustain a rib fracture, punctured lung or cardiac contusion, all potential complications of external cardiac massage. After his loading dose of dilantin he was cautioned not to stop his medication again without consulting his physician. I commended his co-worker for her helping spirit but warned her in no uncertain terms to get appropriate training before attempting anything like this again.

In summary the principles of training are:

TRAIN FOR PREDICTED CRISIS
TRAIN FOR GENERIC CRISIS
PRACTICE, PRACTICE, PRACTICE

EXERCISE

Sign up for a training course in a crisis management related skill. An American Heart Association sponsored course in CPR would be a good choice. There are many others to choose from including courses in driving, wilderness survival skills, self-defense and physical conditioning. The main point here is to gain firsthand experience with the concepts of training. Take notes during the course. Pay attention to the techniques and skills involved in the act of training. How would you employ them to train yourself and others in other crisis management skills? You don't necessarily need a teaching certificate. The general practice in medical school is, "See one, do one, teach one."

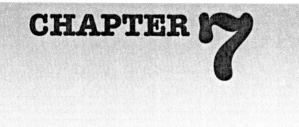

PROBLEM SOLVING

Murphy's Law is a well-known popular maxim. Simply stated, "If anything can go wrong it will." Although this is not technically an actual law of nature it strikes many of us as a useful, often humorous, explanation of everyday events. The origin of Murphy's law is somewhat less well known. Edward A. Murphy Jr. was an engineer working on rocket sled experiments for the US Airforce in 1949. His original statement related to a particular experiment in which each of a series of 16 accelerometer sensors was glued to its mounting backwards. Several days after his initial utterance an adaptation of his comment was quoted at a news conference by Major John Paul Stapp, a pioneer in the science of collision investigation.

Murphy's Law was immediately adopted by aerospace engineers and was indicative of the thinking responsible for the redundant "backup systems" which played a significant role in the success of America's space program and related engineering efforts. Subsequently Murphy's Law was adopted by popular culture, eventually earning mention in Webster's Dictionary in 1958.

How is this relevant to crisis management? Murphy's Law addresses things going wrong, otherwise known as problems. If we view crisis management within the format of problem solving, as a problem or series of problems to be solved, we can apply the various techniques of problem solving to crisis management. This provides us with additional tools to utilize in our crisis situation.

What then are the techniques or tools of problem solving?

Pose a problem. Entertain multiple competing ideas. Experiment and make observations. Continue to search until a useful solution is found.

POSE A PROBLEM
ENTERTAIN IDEAS
EXPERIMENT
MAKE OBSERVATIONS
FIND USEFUL SOLUTIONS

This all sounds very scientific. In fact it is quite similar to the basic **scientific method** of investigation. To phrase it in more vernacular form: When a crisis presents you with a problem, brainstorm to think of the factors responsible and potential solutions. Select the best possible solution by observation, experimentation and reasoning using your best judgment.

If you can equate crisis management to problem solving in your thought process then when a crisis occurs you will naturally and automatically think in terms of, "What is the problem and how can it be solved?" It is this automatic response that we seek to trigger. This can be accomplished through practice and training. It will help build confidence, defuse panic and allay fear.

Let's take a simple real life problem and work through it to a solution. Your son goes away to college. Upon arrival he discovers that he really needs the use of his bicycle on the huge campus. Of course he didn't think of this when you drove him to college the week before, though he did think to bring his stereo. The campus is 1000 miles away.

First let's refer to our definition to see if this is even a crisis. Are the elements of a crisis: **change, conflict, decision, consequences, uncertainty and fear,** present or not? You may decide it is not a crisis at all. If on the other hand you decide it is one, it is certainly a minor crisis. This immediately defuses some of the pressure imposed on you by your son. Now let's review the basic problem solving tools and proceed to solve the problem.

POSE A PROBLEM
ENTERTAIN IDEAS
EXPERIMENT
MAKE OBSERVATIONS / GATHER INFORMATION
FIND USEFUL SOLUTIONS

The problem has been posed by your son. "How can I get my bicycle?" Let's entertain some ideas. Idea #1 might be walking is good exercise and he really doesn't need a bicycle. Idea #2 might be to give him money to buy a used bicycle for use on campus. Another might be to put his bicycle on your car's bike rack and drive the 2000 mile round trip to his school. Proceed to "brainstorm" and list additional ideas of your own. Next, experiment mentally with the various theories, following each scenario to its logical conclusion. Make observations regarding each in turn and use your judgment to select the most useful solution.

Eventually you decide that shipping the bicycle to your son is the most useful solution. At this point you need to gather more information. How do I ship a bicycle? Where can I get a suitable box? How can I get the bicycle into the box? How much does it cost? Which shippers will handle it safely and economically? Each of these in turn may present an additional problem to be solved.

After obtaining a bicycle box from a bike shop for free since they throw them away after receiving shipment, you partially disassemble the bike, pack it in the box, lug it to the post office and ship it off to your son. There will of course be problems in shipping, but nothing you can't handle with your newfound problem solving ability. Refer back to Murphy's Law. You insured the shipment didn't you?

There are of course other useful problem solving strategies. Don't overlook the creative approach. Utilize imagination, intuition, or contemplation. "Brainstorming" is often a good team strategy where a group throws out ideas, free associates and just says whatever comes to mind. Once a solution is decided upon, take direct action. Additional problem solving techniques include looking for "canned solutions", seeking advice, or consultation with experts.

You now know the basic problem solving techniques: **pose a problem, entertain ideas,**

experiment, make observations, find useful solutions. Write them on a 3X5 card. Keep it in your wallet and practice, practice, practice. When a crisis occurs your reaction should be to approach it as another problem to be solved.

MISTAKES

Corollary to problem solving is another facet of crisis management, dealing with mistakes. The appropriate question is not, "What do I do **if** I make a mistake?", but rather, "What do I do **when** I make a mistake?" The distinction is important. **Mistakes will be made**, both by you and by others. We know this as certainly as we know that **a crisis will occur**. We are all human and prone to err. When you make a mistake it is important to do the following:

ADMIT THE MISTAKE TO YOURSELF
CONSIDER PUBLIC ADMISSION
APOLOGIZE
RECTIFY THE MISTAKE
DO NOT REPEAT IT

The first principle of managing mistakes is perhaps the most important. If we do not recognize that we have made a mistake and admit it to ourselves none of the other steps can follow. We risk compounding the mistake and allowing it to grow and assume a life of its own. The mistake may in fact grow to become its own crisis. It may even become a bigger crisis than the one it originated from. A perfect example of this was the Watergate Crisis in 1974. A burglary of Democratic Party offices authorized by lower level managers was allowed to become a major crisis that ultimately toppled a sitting president and changed the course of political history. This occurred because Richard Nixon, fearful of adverse publicity, refused to admit a mistake. He refused first to admit it to himself and then to the public. His cover-up of the Watergate burglary became a much bigger crisis than the burglary itself. He could have terminated the crisis if he had admitted a mistake had been made by his subordinates, punished those responsible and apologized to the American people.

Next, **consider public admission**. Why do I say, "consider"? Isn't it always best to own up to our mistakes immediately and publicly? The answer is ordinarily yes. How we do so however, often depends on circumstances. Allow me to clarify by the use of examples.

Performers are trained to always continue their performance despite the most glaring error or mistake. There is no reason to stop and draw further attention to it. Many observers may not even notice the mistake due to momentary inattention or lack of familiarity with the technical aspects of the performance. Why ruin the show by drawing unnecessary attention to an error? Afterwards, if questioned about the error, the best course would be to admit to it and apologize. Certainly the performer would want to learn from the error and try hard not to repeat it, probably through additional preparation and training. However, most people respect the integrity of a performer who presses on despite an obvious error.

To cite a medical example, prior to a particularly difficult procedure a physician will often admit to the patient that there is a very real risk of failure. In my experience this is much more ethical and responsible than to cover up the potential risks the patient faces. As I tell my medical students, "If you predict the worst and the best happens you are a miracle worker. If you predict the worst and the worst happens you are a prophet. If you predict the best and the worst happens you are a bum. Would you rather be a bum or get to choose between being a prophet or a miracle worker?" If a mistake does occur it is better to be forthright and explain what happened to the patient and the family, rather than have them find out themselves. Otherwise they may then believe you have even more to hide. Set yourself up for success in spite of mistakes. You will make them.

Apology is almost universally appropriate in the face of a mistake. It should be immediate and sincere. It needs to be accompanied by assurances of future good faith efforts or even the offer of compensation when appropriate.

Why is apology so difficult? Possibly because it seems to somehow wound our ego and make us feel less masterful, adequate or competent. Perhaps we are embarrassed. Often we don't think we are wrong. This may be failure to admit a mistake. Sometimes it is because of advice that apology is an admission of guilt and can be used against us.

Get over these feelings. Become humbler. Understand that everyone is human and makes mistakes. Get good legal advice when necessary and use your own judgment in this regard. Often times the plaintiff in litigation will say that all he wanted at first was an apology. Practice apologizing. Apologize to your spouse, friends and associates—even to strangers on the street.

There's no need to become obsequious, or inappropriate. Avoid destructive second-guessing and self-recrimination. Be sincere, try hard to understand the other person's point of view and recognize your mistakes. Vow not to repeat them. Practice, practice, practice. It will make you a better crisis manager and possibly a better person. Once we have recognized a mistake, admitted it to ourselves, decided to disclose it, apologized and vowed not to repeat it, how do we go about correcting or rectifying it? This relates back to the previous discussion of problem solving. A mistake is just another kind of problem to be solved.

PROBABILITY

Before leaving the topics of Murphy's law and mistakes, we should touch briefly on the concept of probability. Once again we will attempt to bring some science, in this case mathematics, to the topic at hand. This can be a real eye opener in terms of what to expect in certain situations.

Let's assume the probability of a given event is 50%. This means half of the time we will get result A and the other half of the time result B. For purposes of this example we will use the flip of a coin coming up heads as result A. The probability of two such events in a row is the product of the individual probabilities, the two multiplied together. So, in the example of a coin flip, the probability of two heads in a row is 0.5 X 0.5 = 0.25 or 25%, a one in four chance. The probability of three heads in a row is 0.5 X 0.5 X 0.5 = 0.125 or 12.5%, a one in eight chance.

For purposes of illustration, we have formulated a four-step plan in response to a potential crisis. Through good planning, superior personnel and outstanding training we feel confident the chances of each step being successfully executed approach 90%. If we accept these parameters then the probability of the entire plan working flawlessly is 0.9 X 0.9 X0.9 X 0.9

= 0.66 or 66%. This is better than 50/50, but we still have a one third chance of failure, or at least only partial success. If the plan has 10 steps our probability of flawless execution falls to 35%.

Another interesting calculation relates to the probability of failure of a particular device or piece of equipment. Assume that we have a device with a 1% risk of failure on any given day. This would seem to be fairly reliable. Now lets assume we are relying on 100 such devices. The cumulative probability of failure increases with the number of devices according to the formula $CP = 1 - (0.99 \times 0.99 \times 0.99...$multiplied out 100 times). If you do the math this works out to be about 63%. Therefore on any given day the probability that at least one of these devices will fail is more likely than not. If the math does not make you feel humble go back and reread Murphy's Law.

This is another good reason to adhere to the **kiss principle,** already introduced in the chapter on crisis planning. Keep it simple, stupid. The fewer steps there are in the plan, the fewer pieces of equipment and number of people you are reliant upon, the greater your probability of success, all other things being equal. Complicated multi-step plans may look elegant on paper, but often they do not work well in real life. Seek simplicity to minimize mistakes. At the same time don't neglect considering them in planning because **mistakes will occur.**

AVOIDING MISTAKES

Now that we are more tolerant of mistakes, why should we worry about avoiding them? The answer is that certain mistakes are associated with unacceptably severe consequences. These are so called and sometimes truly, **fatal mistakes**. One certainly hopes to never make a fatal mistake even once. If the mistake involves your own personal situation it may be quite literally your last mistake. Since it can be somewhat difficult to learn about fatal mistakes from personal experience and since experience is a key to the proper development of good judgment, how do you then learn about fatal mistakes? The answer is by studying somebody else's crisis. This is properly done in the crisis resolution phase, which as we know is also the pre-crisis phase. In medicine we refer to this as an "autopsy" or "post-mortem" exam. The purpose is to look for an undiagnosed cause of death.

To learn how not to make a fatal mistake you must imagine yourself in someone else's crisis. Think about what they did and what you would do differently to achieve a better outcome. If this is a potential crisis of significant probability it behooves you to **plan, prepare** and **train** for it. In the case of a potentially fatal outcome even a relatively small probability that this crisis will occur may be very significant.

A medical example of a low probability but potentially life threatening crisis is a condition called epiglottitis. If I see 100 patients with a sore throat, perhaps one of them will have epiglottitis—swelling of the covering flap that protects the windpipe when you swallow. Failure to recognize this condition could be a **fatal mistake,** resulting in death by asphyxiation. How do I avoid making this mistake? I look for the signs and symptoms every time I examine a patient complaining of sore throat. Is it worth looking down 100 throats to make the diagnosis once? What would you think if you were the patient with epiglottitis?

PROBLEM

A particularly good example of problem solving is illustrated by the flight of Apollo 13. On April 11, 1970 at 1:13 PM CST the Apollo 13 space capsule blasted off from the Kennedy Space Center in Florida atop a huge Saturn 5 rocket. It was many years since the first manned space flight. Earlier Apollo missions had made even landings on the moon appear routine. The American public wasn't very interested in what seemed at first to be just another trip to the moon.

On April 13 at 9:07 PM the routine nature of the flight changed suddenly and dramatically when the spaceship shook with a bang and a sudden jolt. A yellow warning light flashed. An alarm sounded signaling loss of power in one of the two main electrical panels. The words of Captain Jim Lovell beamed down to earth, "Houston, we've had a problem." Actually, as both the astronauts and the ground controllers in Houston quickly realized, Apollo 13 had several problems simultaneously. There was a partial loss of electrical power. The instruments were indicating a low reading in one of their two oxygen tanks. The space capsule began to wobble uncontrollably, creating another problem with the distribution of solar heat and threatening to create a navigation system failure. Not only would the moon landing have to be canceled, for agonizing hours it appeared as though the remaining resources of the Apollo spacecraft might not be adequate to bring the astronauts home alive.

As commander of the spacecraft, Lovell needed to rapidly assess his situation. He needed to know the cause of the problem and whether the problem was with the sensors giving abnormal readings or the actual systems they monitored. He looked at the readout for his #2 oxygen tank. It was zero. Then he looked out the window. What he saw out the small side window of the ship was a white cloud of gas venting from the spacecraft—venting out into the emptiness of space.

Although this story is a wonderful example of many if not all aspects of crisis management, for our purposes here we will focus on the techniques of problem solving illustrated. Readers interested in a more in depth review are encouraged to read Jim Lovell's book, "Lost Moon", which gives an interesting and thorough report of this event.

NASA managers and the crew of the spaceship dealt with this crisis from the standpoint of a problem solving exercise. First they assessed the situation and listed all the problems needing solution (**pose a problem**). Then they assembled as much brainpower as they could bring to bear looking for solutions (**entertain ideas**). By virtue of the structure of the space program people were already organized into teams which each worked on an individual problem or set of problems. They set about solving these problems through careful thought, data collection and analysis, calculation and innovation (**experiment, make observations**). The solutions to individual problems then had to be combined, integrated into the fabric of the larger problem and implemented (**find useful solutions**). The complexity of the tasks involved made their success seem nothing short of miraculous.

The crew of Apollo 13 was able to survive by transferring into the intact lunar landing module (LEM) and conserving the scarce resources available. Then, just prior to re-entry, they transferred back into the crippled command module, jettisoned the LEM and returned to earth.

EXERCISE

Consider a fatal crisis from a recent news report. Choose one that seems to have some applicability to your personal situation, perhaps a drowning or a fire related death. Are you prepared for such a situation? Do you have a personal plan and the requisite training? If not, what better time to plan and prepare for this than now, in the pre-crisis stage?

IN CASE OF EMERGENCY

TURN TO THE NEXT PAGE

ASSESS

DECIDE

ACT

The management of crisis is, in a sense, as simple as the three words immediately above. How to understand and utilize these simple concepts will be dealt with in more detail in chapter 8.

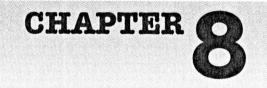

CHAPTER 8

EVENT MANAGEMENT

You've tried hard to prevent this crisis. You planned for it. You prepared and trained. Despite your best efforts a crisis has occurred. You predicted it didn't you? Well not exactly. You didn't predict this particular crisis at this particular time. To make matters worse, this is a major crisis at a very bad time. Are you sure it's a major crisis? How are you feeling? Do you feel overwhelmed, taken completely by surprise, unable to cope, on the verge of panic? What about your physical state? Is your mouth dry, like it's stuffed with cotton? Do you feel a lump in your throat? Are you angry, weak, depressed, confused, numb? Yes, this is a major crisis all right.

So, what do you do now? Is this a predicted crisis with previous planning, preparation and training? Proceed with confidence to implement your plan secure in the knowledge that you have done your best to influence the outcome of this crisis.

Is this a recurrent crisis, one that has happened to you or others in the past? If so, utilize the lessons learned and implement those strategies previously proven effective. At the same time learn from past mistakes and avoid repeating them. Draw upon the experience, skill and knowledge of those who have "been there before."

Is this a new, unexpected crisis, one for which you have no specific plan? If so, draw upon the generic skills you have learned and practiced when managing previous crisis situations. Gather relevant information and weigh it carefully. Consider the various possible courses of action and decide on one or more. Act boldly to implement your plans.

The keystones of effective crisis management are:

ASSESSMENT
DECISION
ACTION

ASSESSMENT

Be cold, hard and objective in your **assessment**. View the situation as if you were a totally detached third party observer. Put aside emotion. Distance yourself from anger, fear, or elation. Avoid wishful thinking. Eliminate bias. Seek other opinions.

You must be objective. What is really happening? What are the possible outcomes? What is likely to happen? What needs to be done to affect a positive outcome? Gather as much relevant information as possible in the time available.

The two major classes of information are subjective and objective. Subjective information has been filtered by a person. It contains personal prejudices, bias and is colored by past experience. It may in fact be accurate or valuable, as long as you understand it is influenced by its source. For example the statement, "It was a very hot day," is subjective information. Objective information on the other hand is, theoretically, without bias. "The air temperature was 99 degrees Fahrenheit," would be an objective restatement of the same fact. Whenever possible obtain objective information and decide for yourself.

In the medical realm **assessment** is of paramount importance. Without an accurate diagnosis appropriate therapy is difficult or impossible. The Advanced Trauma Life Support Course, developed by the American College of Surgeons and taught to emergency physicians and trauma surgeons, stresses this fact. Before acting in any trauma case we are taught first to do a "primary survey" to look for any life threatening emergencies. These are then acted upon immediately in order to stabilize the patient before undertaking the more detailed and time consuming "secondary survey", a comprehensive and thorough review of the entire body for all potential injuries. Without this deliberate, prioritized assessment, it is all too easy to be distracted by an obvious, but non-life-threatening injury, such as an open fracture (with the bone protruding). Such distraction could result in failure to recognize a more serious, but less obvious problem, such as pneumothorax (collapsed lung). Alternatively, in a patient with multiple injuries it would be easy to completely overlook a relatively minor problem such as a broken foot, that might cause disability later on.

Assessment skills, like any others, can be acquired and improved through training and practice. Take the time to assess carefully before making decisions. How much time you take to assess the situation depends on how much time you have. In a life threatening situation you may literally only have seconds. In the earlier story of the falling ladder there was only a fraction of a second. In most cases, however, there is ample time for a careful assessment.

A good example of assessment and the lack of assessment, was provided by a patient who rushed into our emergency room one day. He was surrounded by family members, several of whom were screaming hysterically at us to do something. The patient was covered with blood from head to toe. Without stopping for the triage nurse they burst into the department, demanding immediate attention. The nurses ushered the patient into an empty room, laid him flat on a gurney and immediately began installing an IV. No one, including the patient, was coherent enough to give a history. I instructed the nurses to take vital signs and begin cleaning him up to see if we could find the source of all that blood.

Once the blood had been wiped from his face and head the source became obvious. There was a small artery spurting bright red blood like a fountain from the top of his head. Direct pressure from a gloved index finger stopped the blood flow as if turning off a faucet. His pulse was rapid but his blood pressure was OK.

After he calmed down he was able to tell us the story. He had bumped his head on the sharp corner of a cabinet in the kitchen. The scalp wound by chance opened a small artery which began to shower him with blood. Somewhat dazed from the thump by the cabinet he stumbled into the living room where his surprised family members, seeing his face covered with blood, panicked. Their terrified reaction in turn frightened the patient and they all piled into the family car together and raced to the hospital without a thought as to what was actually happening.

He was young and otherwise healthy. The bleeding stopped with direct pressure and a pressure dressing was applied. The wound was so trivial it didn't even require a stitch. After a liter of IV fluid he felt much better and was able to go home, following a brief bedside lesson in first aid for bleeding.

DECISION

In a true crisis you must make a **decision** expeditiously in order to act. In retrospect, it may not turn out to be the best possible decision. Later on, in the presence of complete information, a better decision may be possible. But in a crisis we rarely have complete information put before us. More often we are dealing with rumor, supposition, hysteria and confusion. Sift the facts. Assess the situation, then decide. If you cannot devise a reasonable plan seek assistance, preferably from an expert in the field in which the crisis has occurred. In medicine we term this a consultation and we do it all the time. No one can hope to be an expert on everything.

Although on occasion the decision to do nothing may be the best choice, make sure that doing nothing does not involve a greater risk than the risk of action. Be wary of indecision based on fear. To quote Ross Perot, the multimillionaire founder of Electronic Data Systems, "If you go through life worrying about all the bad things that can happen, you soon convince yourself that it's best to do nothing at all." Within the medical model for decision-making we use the concept of differential diagnosis. If a patient presents to the emergency department with chest pain, like the patient in chapter one for example, emergency physicians make a mental list of all the possible causes. These might include such other processes as pneumonia, a fractured rib, a peptic ulcer, or several other disease processes which can cause chest pain. We then proceed to further assess the situation by making observations (physical examination), gathering additional data (blood tests, x-rays, an EKG) and by asking the patient more specific questions (history). These then help us to "rule in" or "rule out" the various possibilities. Once we have gathered as much data and information as possible under the circumstances, we decide upon the most likely diagnosis. When the diagnosis is established we are ready to act.

Often after a careful assessment is performed the decision becomes obvious, as you saw in the example of arterial bleeding immediately above. If this is not the case you may need to utilize more formal decision-making tools. You will learn about these tools a little further on in this chapter.

ACTION

It goes without saying that you will be better able to act if you have previously **planned, prepared** and **trained**. Action becomes straightforward if all you need to do is apply the appropriate algorithm, open to the page in the cookbook, or apply lessons you have learned and drilled in training.

Be warm, flexible and enthusiastic in your **action**s. Enthusiasm is contagious. Infect your team with it. **Think clearly and act decisively** to work toward the best possible outcome. Be flexible enough to alter or modify the plan if it isn't working or if the situation changes. This is the time to pull out all the stops, focus your complete attention and work diligently on the task at hand. You may not get a second chance. At this point you must exert maximum effort both mentally and physically. Never give up.

PULL OUT ALL THE STOPS
FOCUS YOUR ATTENTION
NEVER GIVE UP

PULL OUT ALL THE STOPS

A word here about maximal effort. Never underestimate the possible. The challenge of a crisis situation may seem totally daunting, beyond your own, your team's or even human capacity. Don't let this stop you from trying. First of all the limits of human capacity are way beyond what most people think they are. Who in the early 1960's thought we would ever land a man on the moon? It happened within a decade.

Even a few years ago, who thought Mt. Everest could be climbed without oxygen or by anyone other than highly skilled professional mountaineers. Everest has now been climbed without oxygen and people without extensive mountaineering experience have been guided to the top. Haven't you ever pushed the limits and accomplished something you didn't think you could? You will not succeed every time you try this or you are seriously underestimating your capabilities. You will, however, succeed some of the time. You won't get a chance to be lucky unless you assume some risks. Don't be afraid to **pull out all the stops** and "go for it" in a crisis situation.

DECISION MAKING TOOLS

In a true crisis isn't it worth taking the risk? To answer this question let's introduce the concept of **risk / benefit analysis**. What are you risking by attempting the task in question? Are you risking a good night's sleep, upsetting a co-worker, your boss, or your spouse? Are you risking embarrassment, or are you risking your business, your life or someone else's life? What is the potential benefit or gain from the attempt? What is the likelihood of success or failure?

Once we have considered and tried to quantify these three factors, **risks, benefits and probability of success,** we can make a decision. Of course this is not an exact science. The risks and benefits are only those we, or our team members, can think of at the time. The probabilities are only a guess based upon experience. Be careful of wishful thinking here. But what's the alternative? Remember this is a crisis. Giving up is not an option. We have to **do something.**

Let's set this up as a **decision matrix**.

DECISION MATRIX

RISKS	BENEFITS	PROBABILITY (success)	ACTION
Minimal	Great	>75%	Do It
Death	Moderate	50%	Don't Do It
Moderate	Moderate	50%	Consider

Customize this construct. Set it up any way you want. Decide what you consider an acceptable probability, risk, benefit, etc. The point is to develop a useful decision-making tool.

If your analysis leads you to believe a certain action is not worth the risk, consider doing something else. We all make many decisions every day. It is usually not worth going to the trouble to draw up a decision matrix. It can be very useful, however, for major or difficult decisions. In a crisis situation where decision-making is often critical it can be very helpful. It can also be helpful later if you find yourself having to justify or explain why you did what you did.

Sometimes we are faced with complex decisions involving multiple parameters that seem to defy conventional analysis. Personally I have found that giving the decision some time, otherwise known as "sleeping on it", can help greatly to clarify a decision. This strategy can be applied to decisions where time is not as critical but the stakes are great, such as whether to get married for instance.

FOCUS YOUR ATTENTION

It is all too easy to become distracted during a crisis. Someone comes to you with a new problem, idea, or issue, which may be minor or even unrelated to the crisis at hand. The immediacy of another person standing in front of you is hard to ignore. Nonetheless it is incumbent upon the crisis manager to exclude unrelated, trivial, or less urgent matters in order to **focus your attention** on the crisis. You must tactfully explain, in brief, why you're going to put this new issue " on the back burner" until the true crisis is past. In a real emergency you may choose to simply ignore the other person. If subsequent events don't justify this in his eyes you can always explain and apologize later. How do you decide what to ignore and what to focus your attention on? **Judgment**, based on experience practicing the principles of crisis management.

The emergency room is again a good example for this issue of **focus**. Often the ER is a maelstrom of sights, sounds and people, all trying to grab your attention at once. An experienced emergency physician knows when to focus his concentration on a single patient or problem and yet has to be alert to the appearance of a new, even more urgent situation. Various strategies can be adopted, such as letting one physician concentrate on a single sick patient for a period of time while a second doctor sees multiple patients who are less urgent. The staff can be directed to only contact the doctor in the case of an even more urgent patient arriving.

NEVER GIVE UP

What if you cannot regain control or implement a workable plan? Focus on survival. What must be done to keep you, your family, or your organization alive? **Never give up**. The alternative to continuing your efforts is failure. Why not persist? Make tenacity your watchword.

MANAGEMENT

In any acute crisis event there are a multitude of things to be managed. The most important of these include the following:

COMMUNICATIONS
EMOTIONS
STRESS
MEDIA
EXPECTATIONS
PEOPLE
EVENTS

COMMUNICATIONS

Time and again in the course of interviewing the participants in a crisis, I have listened to them stress the critical role played by **communications.** Your capabilities in the vital realm of communications, or lack thereof, can make or break you in a crisis situation.

Set up a "command post" with the best available communication facility. Multiple phone lines may be necessary. This might be an office, your home, a cellular phone, or a physically prominent place such as a hilltop. You will need to communicate swiftly and effectively with your team, oftentimes the opposition, other involved parties, news media and the public. Keep a list of their names, phone numbers, pager numbers and other modes of contact. Make sure everyone who "needs to know" has access to the command post, especially the phone number. Exclude everyone else to avoid overloading your communication capacity. Provide for obvious contingencies, such as a power outage, loss of phone service, cell phone service, or even the command post itself.

EMOTIONS

Emotions, your own and those of others, must be managed intensively in any crisis. It is difficult or even impossible to think clearly and act decisively if you are distracted or overwhelmed by strong emotions. It is human to feel grief, fear, pity, or elation in response to situational stimuli. During an acute event however, you must temporarily put these emotions aside in order to function and concentrate on dealing with the crisis. Emotions must not be allowed to cloud your judgment or prevent you from timely, rational response. At the same time you cannot allow yourself to appear cold, callous and unfeeling to those around you. This is not an easy concept to master. It may require significant thought, practice and the elicitation of feedback from others.

An example of this is a cardiac arrest code where things are not going well. The physician may begin to develop the sick, sinking feeling that the patient is not going to be resuscitated. In fact, contrary to what we see on television, the majority of patients brought to the ER in cardiac arrest do not survive. Emotions may be running especially high if the patient is relatively young, or a trauma victim with no serious history of disease. It is difficult to lose any patient, but much more so a patient not previously expected to die. At some point the physician in charge needs to make the decision to cease all resuscitation efforts and pronounce the patient dead. There are other patients waiting for treatment. A major proportion of the ER's resources and personnel are tied up in the code. Yet often the code will proceed long past the point that all hope of success has been lost.

It is necessary to put **emotion** aside and make a dispassionate, objective decision. If all steps of the appropriate algorithm have been followed to their logical conclusion and all efforts have been without response from the patient in the form of vital signs (pulse, blood pressure, efforts at breathing) then the code must be called and the patient pronounced dead. It is always a difficult thing to do. Confidence that the patient has been managed correctly, according to accepted algorithms and protocols makes it bearable. In order to successfully manage emotions we must: **have a plan, focus on it's execution** and **practice.**

Managing the **emotions** of those around you can be even more problematic. Whenever possible address emotional issues in the context of preparation and training. If this has not occurred in the pre-crisis phase be prepared to deal with emotions. You may need to offer support or encouragement to others, or to lead by example. By appearing calm, confident and in control of your own emotions and by directly confronting hysterical or dangerously irrational behavior, you will set the emotional tone for other members of your team.

Fear is a primal emotion. It can often take the form of a "fight or flight" survival response. The intense feelings produced are accompanied by a physiologic release of adrenaline. This hormone acts as a potent stimulant, speeding up the heart rate and respiration, energizing muscles and heightening awareness. Uncontrolled, this response can be overwhelming in a negative way, leading to irrational action or inaction. If controlled or "channeled" however, the fight or flight response to fear, or for that matter to anger or other strong emotions, can provide us with seemingly superhuman physical power and mental focus.

How can we channel fear, anger, or other strong emotions? You should be able to answer this question by now. Practice, practice, practice. Start with a minor episode, anger over a comment or slight at work by an associate. Immediately focus on channeling this energy into a positive response. Think of something positive to do. It may be directed towards the person or circumstance that caused the emotion, or totally unrelated. The important thing is to seize and channel that energy to a useful purpose. Once you experience what this feels like do it at every opportunity. It may even make you more productive. When a crisis occurs recognize your emotions. Then channel them into positive action, just as you have been doing in practice.

We have all seen this phenomenon as a reaction to grief in the aftermath of a tragic death. Often the survivors will channel their grief into a related cause or crusade. Examples include the Mothers Against Drunk Driving organization, crusades to erect railroad-crossing gates, memorial scholarship funds and efforts to pass a law designed to prevent future tragedies.

Another useful tool in the management of fear is the experience of, quite simply, doing the things you fear. Start with small things and work your way up. Try your hand at public speaking. Volunteer for a leadership position. Take prudent risks in pursuit of personal and organizational goals. Don't be afraid to fail. Avoid obviously dangerous things. The idea is to prepare yourself to deal with crisis, not seek it out. If you make a habit of facing up to fearful situations and people on a regular basis it will not be as difficult when a crisis occurs. When you are confronted by real, palpable, naked fear, the fact that you have successfully faced down fear in the past can give you the confidence to **think clearly** and **act decisively**.

Another technique for handling fear is to **have no time for fear.** It has impressed me time and again when discussing harrowing episodes, that often people deny they experienced any fear at all. Typically they do not consider themselves heroes. The usual comment is that they weren't afraid at the time because they were too busy managing the situation to think about fear. Most often this management response was automatic and was a result of previous **planning, preparation and training**. An example of this can sometimes be seen in motor vehicle collisions or other rapidly occurring events. Finally, the technique of **acceptance** may be useful in the face of fear. Recognize the worst possible outcome. Can you somehow accept or come to terms with it? It might not even be as bad as you first presumed. This is not the same as giving up. You still must try your very best to improve upon the worst possible result. However, if you can accept that the worst might occur and get beyond it, you will be better able to deal with events and control your fear.

One of the most heroic examples of the power of **acceptance** involved a patient who developed an incurable cancer. As an intelligent person, he had asked the difficult questions of his doctors and had done his own research. Although he resolved not to give up and continued to pursue therapy with the hope of a cure, in his heart he knew it was likely he would die. He was a relatively young man with a wife and children. He had a successful career and was active in community affairs and religious organizations. After initial treatment he was able to continue his professional activities for a time. Gradually, as the disease progressed, he was forced to withdraw one at a time from his various activities. During this time he seemed at peace with himself. Always positive and upbeat, he had resolved to do as much as he was able for as long as he could. When at last his strength gave out, he died quietly at home in bed, surrounded by his family.

Whenever you are confronted by fear or other strong emotions, utilize the techniques you have learned: **channeling, doing the things you fear, having no time for fear** and **acceptance.** Then, **formulate a plan** and **focus on its execution**.

STRESS

Stress can be defined as, "emotional or intellectual strain or tension". By this definition I am purposely excluding physical forms of stress, such as extreme heat or cold and focusing on mental stress. Stress is a fact of life and can be neatly divided into eustress (good stress) and distress (bad stress). Good or bad, stress can color our perception of reality and affect our ability to perform in time of crisis. A classic stress inducing situation is one in which a person is granted limited authority and yet given total responsibility. An example from the world of business would be assuming responsibility for a department without being given any budgetary or personnel authority. Overwhelming stress can cause the most patient among us to "snap" and say or do ugly things we much regret later.

Stress is often present in a crisis situation. You are being called upon to make critical decisions, perform difficult tasks and manage a multitude of problems. Of course you're under stress. How do you manage it?

Stress is often induced or accompanied by a feeling of being out of control. You have lost control of the situation, of events, perhaps even of your own emotions. The first thing you must do is regain control. Sometimes this is as simple as taking a deep breath and composing yourself. You may need to stop what you're doing and think about what is happening around you. Often you can start by regaining control of your immediate environment. Eliminate unnecessary physical agents of stress such as noise pollution, extremes of temperature, hunger, lack of sleep. Turn down the volume on the telephone ringers. Close the doors and windows to eliminate extraneous noise. Banish unneeded people from the room. Make sure both you and your team have adequate rest and are not skipping meals. Often surgeons play soothing music in the operating room and control the temperature carefully for maximum comfort, to minimize stress. These things may seem petty, minor details in a crisis, but they can negatively impact your ability to **think clearly** and **act decisively**.

Another technique of dealing with stress is through the maintenance of your sense of humor. It may be tremendously stress relieving to laugh out loud at yourself, the situation, or the total nightmarish quality of events. This may explain the so-called "black humor" sometimes in evidence under the most horrendous circumstances. Be careful where and in front of whom you do this. It may easily be misinterpreted. The safest method is to keep the jokes to yourself and do any laughing in total privacy.

Once the crisis is past, deal with residual stress through evaluation, feedback and reassurance in the crisis resolution phase.

MEDIA

The time to establish a connection with the media is in the pre-crisis stage. Why would we want to do this? It's time consuming, may involve the expense of a public relations person, is often frustrating and may be a complete waste of time and energy. As a private person there is no reason to do this. As a public person or the representative of a large organization there is every reason to. Remember, a crisis will occur. When it does you will look better in the media if you have planned, prepared, practiced and trained. It also won't hurt if you are personally familiar with the media person interviewing you.

Get your PR person to arrange a TV or radio interview. Write an article on a topic of importance in your industry and have it published in the local press. This is a lot easier than you may think. The number of media outlets has multiplied exponentially in recent years with the advent of cable and the internet. They are all looking constantly for content. It's tremendously useful to get the proper coaching and see what you look like on television or sound like on the radio. Seeing your article in print is an ego boosting experience. The feedback from others is important to your development of ideas. All of this will be good preparation for being thrust into the media spotlight during a crisis.

Following the 1990 Amtrak rail disaster in Boston I was interviewed by ABC News. I came across much better on television as a result of doing a routine interview relating to flu shots, with the same reporter, just a few months before.

Be honest and forthright in your statements to the media. If you want them on your side you must maintain credibility. This doesn't prevent you from presenting events in the most favorable light or declining to answer questions on sensitive issues, but your facts must be correct and your statements truthful.

EXPECTATIONS

In order to manage expectations you must first of all know what they are. Take a moment to ask yourself, "What do I expect the outcome of this event to be? What would be the best possible outcome? What would be the worst?" Ask the same questions of the other members of your team, interested parties, experts in the field, anyone whose opinions might be of value.

Now that you have a range of expectations you can proceed to manage them. First of all address your own expectations. Which, in the range of outcomes, would be satisfactory to you? Assess the probability of a favorable result. Come to grips with the potential of failure or the worst outcome. Think about what you will do and how you will react in each eventuality. This is not to say that you won't still do your best to obtain the optimal outcome. But if, due to forces beyond your control, the worst happens, at least you are mentally prepared. With a thorough assessment of your chances and knowledge of the various possibilities you are also better prepared to make decisions.

Once you have managed your own expectations, what about the expectations of others? Think back for a moment to the chapter on problem solving. Remember the three choices I give the medical students in regard to preparing patients? Would you rather be a miracle worker, a prophet, or a bum? This has everything to do with managing expectations. While as a leader one must strive to appear confident and committed, it doesn't make sense to be overly optimistic or to exude confidence in the face of certain disaster. Don't risk destroying your credibility. You will appear much more truthful and more humble, if you admit the possibility of failure exists. You don't want to intentionally mislead people, but it is usually prudent to slightly underestimate your chances of success when addressing the media or a public audience.

It is much better to over-fulfill than to over-promise. Above all, be truthful. Even the worst news can be broached in a tactful and compassionate manner. People will long remember a lie.

One day in the emergency room I saw a woman, accompanied by her adult daughter, with a laceration on the front of her lower leg overlying the shin bone. I was concerned because of the location of the wound, an area of skin tension and potentially poor healing.

In addition the patient was elderly and a diabetic, two additional **risk factors** for a sub-optimal result. I consulted the general surgeon on call who gladly came to see the patient and carefully repaired the wound. As she was discharging the patient I overheard the surgeon describe in glowing terms how well this wound would heal and that there would be no further difficulties with it. After the surgeon left I stepped in briefly to review the patient's instructions. I expressed confidence in the repair done by the surgeon and said I was hopeful the wound would heal rapidly. I cautioned them, however, that because of the risk factors present there was a significant possibility the wound could break down and not heal. I explained the signs of infection and failure to heal and cautioned them to seek medical care right away if they should occur. After the surgeon's sunny sendoff I think they viewed me as an unwelcome storm cloud. I certainly got funny looks from both the patient and her daughter.

Months later, the daughter walked into the emergency room and thanked me. The wound had broken down, become infected, required weeks of antibiotic therapy and ultimately skin grafting. My warning, which had initially been perceived as oddly negative, had alerted them to respond promptly and prepared them to deal with the problem. Rather than anger over a poor outcome, she expressed gratitude for the **management of** her **expectations**.

PEOPLE

The management of people could be the topic of books all by itself. For our purposes in crisis management it is sufficient to say that one manages people through **leadership**. The other important factor relates to the management of large numbers of people. This is accomplished through the **chain of command**. In any enterprise where more than a few people are involved it makes good sense to organize smaller groups into teams, each with its own **team leader**. The leaders than report up the **chain of command** to the CEO, general, chief, president, or whatever designation the overall top guy adopts. Orders and direction likewise can flow back down the chain to the teams or troops.

It is also of paramount importance to choose the very best people you can get in the first place. Then, once they are briefed on the plan, prepared, trained and supplied with the necessary logistical support, often all leadership needs to do is get out of their way and let them do the job.

EVENTS

Management of events is what this whole chapter is about. The point of this particular section is to emphasize that you want to **manage** events rather than simply react to them. On occasion I have run across people with a very fatalistic philosophical viewpoint. I refer to this as the "Whatever Will Be Will Be School of Management". I mention this only to point out that these people do exist. None of them would be reading this book because it is so at odds with their basic philosophy of life. These are people who would not walk any faster to get out of the way of a moving locomotive. A slight exaggeration perhaps, but I swear I've spotted them crossing the street against the traffic light in front of cars.

The vast majority of people are not philosophically opposed to managing events, but a great many of them lack the intellectual tools and know-how to do it. Once you have finished reading this book and doing the exercises you will have the tools and know-how. You must then, you guessed it, **practice, practice, practice**.

My friend Randall Still* tells a story illustrating many of these principles. Randy used to race sailboats on Lake Michigan when he was a student at The University of Chicago.

One Saturday early in the summer he went to Belmont Harbor looking for a spot in someone's racing crew. His goal for that summer was to secure a berth in the Chicago to Mackinac race, a 300-mile, several day race from one end of Lake Michigan to the other. It takes place annually in July. Randy was not planning to race that particular day but when a crew spot was offered on a, "We need you right now. Take it or leave it." basis, he climbed aboard.

Soon he was headed out onto the lake on a 30 foot racing sloop in a brisk wind. The skipper was a distinguished looking middle aged gentleman who obviously had the means to outfit a pricey racing "campaign". The rest of the crew consisted of the helmsman, who appeared to be quite competent at handling the boat, the tactician, who though much younger was a former national champion sailor in the laser class (a smaller sailboat) and two other "deck monkeys" besides himself, who would grind the winches and provide ballast. Randy soon was informed that they often sailed with a crew of 5 and that he had been invited along essentially as extra ballast because it was going to be a "heavy air " day. Randy noted with interest that the boat had a tiller for steering rather than the large wheel more common on big sailboats.

The frenzy of jockeying for position ended with the starting gun and Randy's boat headed off on the first leg of the race, tacking upwind. The wind built up to a steady 25 knots (about 28mph) with gusts to 30 or more. "Ordinarily," Randy thought, "It would be prudent to shorten sail." But this was a race and the skipper seemed quite confident of his boat's capability, so Randy kept his opinion private. Conditions were getting rough. The wave heights were 8 to 10 feet from trough to crest. As the sloop sliced through the seas to windward the other boats were often out of sight, hidden behind a wall of water.

Suddenly, the mast was down! Randy didn't even hear it fall. It seemed to happen instantly and was now lying along the deck in a jumble of ropes, sails and steel wires. Miraculously, no one had been killed, injured or thrown overboard. The entire crew was stunned. The boat, now without steerage, turned sideways to the wind and waves. Then it began to heel over at a 45-degree angle with each foaming wave. Every crewman hung on grimly to avoid being pitched over the side. The engine couldn't be started because one of the lines in the water would surely wrap itself around the propeller shaft.

Randy began to look around for other boats. Certainly a competitor had seen their mast fail and would arrive shortly to offer a tow. But no one was coming. On its side, with no mast, rolling in the waves, the boat offered little profile on the crest and none at all in the trough. All the other sailors were looking upwind towards the mark, not behind them. When Randy realized that no rescue would be coming anytime soon it shook him up. But his next thought was, "What's the worst thing that can happen? No one is hurt. The boat is not sinking. We're drifting downwind across the southern tip of Lake Michigan. Eventually we'll wash up on the beach in Indiana. The lake is shallow and sandy there. The boat may get pounded to pieces by the surf, but we should all get ashore OK." He found this thought somewhat reassuring, although the prospect of spending hours clinging to a pitching deck was not terribly agreeable.

Randy surveyed the scene. The boat was wallowing helplessly without steerage. No rescue seemed imminent. They might not even be missed until after the finish of the race. By that time they would doubtless have drifted many miles downwind, away from Chicago. No one on board could do anything besides hold on. The rolling of the boat with each wave in the heavy chop prevented useful activity of any sort. The tactician was lying in the cockpit, seasick. The deck crew was just hanging on for dear life. No orders of any kind were coming from the skipper. The helmsman had abandoned the tiller, now worthless without the forward momentum of the boat to render the rudder useful.

Or was it? Randy remembered how he had sometimes used the tiller and rudder as a scull or oar to push small sailboats along when the wind died. What could be done with a 30-foot boat weighing several tons? There was only one way to find out. Seizing the tiller with both hands he began "rowing" it back and forth in a manner which caused the boat to turn 90 degrees.

The sailboat was now pointing dead downwind, away from the oncoming waves. It began to slide or surf down the waves, gaining more momentum with each one. Randy glanced at the speedometer. He was making 3 knots with no mast. The boat's top speed, with all sails set was only a little more than 7. Though they were now headed to an even faster rendezvous with the beach in Indiana, the boat had steerage. Its direction was again under the control of the tiller. More importantly, it had stopped lying on its side and the crew immediately got up and began to clear away the wreckage.

Once the lines were cleared from the water the engine could be started and the boat headed back to Belmont Harbor. I understand that later that summer Randy did get to sail in the Mackinac race, which was uneventful.

Let's list the principles of crisis management illustrated by this story.

- **Recognition**: Randy had no difficulty recognizing the situation as a crisis. It was obvious that a critical change had occurred.
- **Planning**: Although he had not planned ahead of time for such a situation, Randy

rapidly formulated a plan on the spot. It was not complicated or detailed. The basic idea was to get the boat stabilized. Once that was accomplished the rest followed naturally.

- **Preparation and Training**: Since he did not predict this particular crisis, Randy had not specifically prepared or trained to cope with it. He had, however, prepared and trained generically in the sailing and handling of a variety of different sailboats. It was this generic preparation and training that enabled him to rapidly formulate and execute a plan that worked.

- **Assessment**: In retelling this story, Randy specifically mentioned the fact that he took stock of the situation for several minutes before formulating a plan and deciding to act. It was the mental discipline of this overall assessment that led to the plan, which more or less, "occurred as an idea" once all the facts were digested.

- **Risk / Benefit Analysis**: There was no time for a formal decision matrix, but Randy nonetheless weighed the risks and benefits and rapidly concluded that the risk of this particular action was less than the risk of doing nothing and the benefits potentially great.

- **Decision**: This risk / benefit analysis rendered the decision to act a virtual "no-brainer" once the plan was conceived.

- **Action**: To his credit, Randy was able to act decisively. He did not hesitate even though he was technically not in command. He saw what was necessary and did it. This usually works well as long as you do the right thing.

But, as in this example, it is often better to do something than to do nothing.

- **Never give up**: Randy could easily have done nothing. He was not in command. It was not his boat. He was not in immediate danger. Instead he chose to **manage events**. He **posed a problem** and came up with a **solution**.
- **Manage emotions / fear**: Randy's assessment was that he was not in imminent danger. By busying himself with the search for a plan as well as his focus on its execution, Randy was able to manage the natural fear in such a situation and facilitate action.
- **Manage people**: Leadership by example was all it took in this case to spark the rest of the crew to act. Once the boat was stabilized the crew's own extensive training "kicked in" and the boat was squared away in short order.

EXERCISE

Make a decision matrix to aid in the making of a significant decision. Practice doing this every day until it becomes a routine and can be done "in your head".

EXERCISE

Practice "channeling". During your regular workout think about something that makes you angry, or perhaps a frightening or dangerous situation. Mentally put yourself in this scenario and let your emotions run wild. Now channel that energy and the released adrenaline, into your workout. It may well be the best workout you've ever had. Have fun with this and practice it regularly when you work out. It's also a great stress reliever.

EXERCISE

Prepare a media "crisis kit" for your organization. It should contain general information regarding the background of your organization and its key players. Outline how your organization has planned, prepared and trained for crisis in a generic sense. Mention your organization's masterful handling of previous crisis situations. Stress its positive role and relationships in the community. Leave room to customize the message to a particular crisis. You are more likely to get positive reporting if you are viewed as helpful and especially so if you are the major source of information.

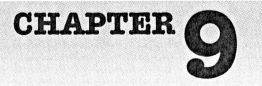

CHAPTER 9

MAJOR CRISIS

On December 12, 1990 at 5:25 a.m. Amtrak train number 66 pulled out of New Haven Connecticut on time, headed for Boston. In the cab of the diesel locomotive were Willis Copeland, an experienced veteran engineer and Richard Abramson, an engineer apprentice. Abramson had begun engineer training school in June of 1990, spent time in the locomotive simulator and ridden as an observer in the cab. On December 10, 1990, after 4 weeks' vacation, he had begun on the job training. He completed two round trip runs between New Haven and Boston on December 10th and 11[th.] . The rest of the train crew included a conductor and two assistants along with the dining car staff.

The engineers boarded the train an hour before departure, reviewed the cab inspection report, checked the radio and tested the air brakes. The train consisted of a two-unit locomotive and ten cars, five of which were passenger cars. Amtrak 66 made its regular station stops at Old Saybrook, New London, Mystic, Westerly, Kingston and Providence, traveling at speeds sometimes slightly exceeding its authorized maximum of 100 miles per hour. The train pulled into the Route 128 station on time at 8:14 a.m. The next stop was Boston's Back Bay Station.

Meanwhile, Massachusetts Bay Transit Authority commuter train 906 was also headed eastbound into Back Bay Station, after pulling out of Stoughton at 7:45 a.m. MBTA 906 was a "push/pull" operation with the locomotive on the rear, westerly end of the train. The engineer rode up front in a separate control car. In between were 6 passenger cars filled with 900 commuters, sipping coffee and reading newspapers, on their way to work in Boston. MBTA 906 pulled into Back Bay Station on track one at 8:23 a.m. and was slowing to a stop.

In preparation for the stop at Back Bay the engineer of Amtrak 66 says he advised his apprentice to begin applying the automatic air-brakes brakes as soon as the Ruggles Street station platform, almost a mile from Back Bay, came into view. At this point Amtrak 66 was churning down the track at 94 miles per hour. The train did not slow sufficiently. It surged eastward, entering the tunnel under Back Bay on track 2, careening around a 9 degree right turn rated for 30 mph at a blistering 76 miles per hour. As they entered the curve the locomotive crew felt the engine tipping to the left toward track one. The last thing they remember seeing was locomotive 1073 of the Massachusetts Bay Transit Authority looming ahead of them.

Two hundred feet east down the welded steel rails from where it entered the curve, Amtrak 66 jumped completely off track two and collided with the MBTA commuter train on track one. Then all hell broke loose. The roar of the collision in the tunnel was deafening. The impact threw the massive engines against the roof of the tunnel and caused the street above Back Bay Station to buckle. Both locomotives and six passenger cars were destroyed. One of the passenger cars was crushed like an accordion. The huge fuel tank on the Amtrak locomotive broke loose and a diesel fueled fire ensued. More than 1000 passengers were thrown around inside the two trains, which now lay twisted together in the heavy smoke filling the train tunnel under Back Bay. At the outset this had all the grim signs of a major mass casualty incident.

The engineer of the MBTA train, thrown to the floor by the collision and not knowing what had happened, radioed an emergency call to his dispatcher to hold all trains. At 8:24 a.m. a passenger from the MBTA train called the 911 operator from the station platform. The operator notified the Boston Police Department, Fire Department and Emergency Medical Services. Also notified were Amtrak, the MBTA police and emergency personnel. Boston EMS immediately dispatched units and activated the EMS disaster plan. Calls went out to all the Boston Trauma Center Hospitals, which in turn each activated their individual disaster plans.

At 8:25 a.m. fire fighters arrived on the scene and immediately ordered additional rescue equipment and ambulances. They then descended into the tunnel and began to search for and rescue injured passengers and crew amid the dense smoke. By 8:28 a.m. the first Boston Emergency Medical Service units arrived on the scene. Triage areas were set up for primary and secondary triage and staging areas established for patient loading and ambulances.

Boston Police arrived at 8:30 a.m., established an inner perimeter and set up a mobile command post, which provided centralized communications for all the various agencies participating in the incident. The fire department together with EMS communication specialists set up a portable radio repeater system. This enabled rescuers in the tunnel to communicate with personnel on the surface.

Two simultaneous rescue operations were mounted from both ends of the train tunnel. Evacuation was hampered by dense smoke from the diesel fire, making it difficult to both see and breath in the tunnel.

One of the assistant MBTA conductors had been standing in the vestibule of the third car just prior to the collision. He heard what he thought was an explosion, was hit by a flying piece of metal and then was thrown from the train to the platform. He picked himself up and, proceeding through dense smoke, directed passengers out the station exit doors and up the stairs.

On the Amtrak train two assistant conductors and an off duty conductor were in the fifth car which had been tipped over and crushed on both ends, jamming the exit doors shut. When the conductors began opening the emergency windows the coach filled with smoke. The conductors continued to open windows and helped passengers out of the coach. They then led the passengers along a catwalk to emergency personnel who guided them to the station platform. The Amtrak conductor was thrown into a counter in the dining car in the crash and hit his head. He got up, proceeded to another passenger coach which had tipped over and began pulling out emergency windows. When the fire department arrived, he and the two Amtrak engineers were evacuated to the hospital. The head dining car attendant was thrown across the car and sustained multiple contusions. He left the empty dining car and squeezed through a small opening into the adjacent coach car where he assisted passengers in getting off the train.

Most of the MBTA passengers were able to use the main exit from platform 2. The Amtrak passengers utilized a tunnel emergency exit because the wrecked locomotives blocked the main tunnel exits. Witnesses described the evacuation as orderly. Passengers were guided through the smoke by train crewmen with flashlights and met by fire fighters and EMS personnel.

MBTA police responded with 41 officers who assisted in the evacuation, crowd control and traffic direction.

Fire and smoke conditions in the tunnel resulted in injuries to 5 EMTs and Paramedics. Exhaust fans were employed to remove the smoke. The diesel fuel fire was extinguished by the Boston Fire Department. The on scene operation including extrication, triage, on scene treatment and transport of 264 patients to 7 hospitals in 18 ambulances and 4 city buses was accomplished in 1 hour and 20 minutes. Miraculously, no one died in the initial collision.

I was in my office in the Emergency Department at St. Elizabeth's Hospital when the nurse in charge called to inform me of the incident. Immediately I activated the hospital disaster plan and all available hospital resources were mobilized. We rapidly cleared the emergency room of non-urgent patients, admitting or discharging those who could not be moved over to the ambulatory clinic. My role, according to the plan, was to serve as triage officer. I stood at the ambulance entrance and quickly assessed each case, assigning incoming patients to the various treatment areas based on the severity of their injuries. It was daytime, we were fully staffed and I was not on clinical duty at the time, so we had an extra doctor. Additional physicians were mobilized from the hospital staff.

We received 17 patients, some of whom are seriously injured. These included the engineer of Amtrak 66 along with the rest of the train's crew. This resulted in media attention for St. Elizabeth's Hospital (and me), with an interview on News Center Five (ABC).

Overall the Amtrak rail "disaster" was a model of successful crisis management. Boston EMS, fire department personnel and police extricated and evacuated 1109 people from the train tunnel. Seven Boston hospitals treated 278 injured patients appropriately and expeditiously. Fourteen were admitted to the hospital. Two hundred sixty-four were evaluated, treated and released. No one died. Post crisis evaluation revealed the on scene triage error rate to be less than 1%. Three interlocking sets of disaster plans (Boston EMS, the Boston Teaching Hospitals' citywide plan and the individual hospitals' disaster plans) worked together almost flawlessly to produce an excellent result. This outcome was not accidental. It was the direct result of years of planning, training and preparation on the part of numerous public and private organizations. A crisis had been predicted, planned, prepared and trained for. No one had known the exact form or timing of the crisis. All that was known was, "**A crisis will occur.**"

One of the passenger cars was crushed like an accordion.

Amtrak Locomotive

MBTA Locomotive with Amtrak Locomotive in the background.

In the aftermath of the collision a Boston firefighter
views the wreckage.

The force of the collision caused the street above to buckle.

Dr. Mark Friedman being interviewed by Terry Schraeder
for ABC News.

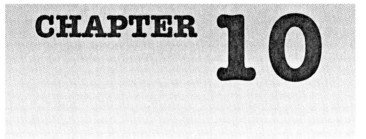

CHAPTER 10

CRISIS RESOLUTION

In medicine we call the crisis resolution phase a "post-mortem". In the military it's referred to as a debriefing. I think I like the military term better. The principle is the same however. Analyze the crisis once it is over. What went wrong? What went right? What was out of our control? What could we do better next time? Which contingencies were we unprepared for? In general it is best to avoid recriminations, second-guessing and blame during this process. Blaming people tends to produce secrecy and defensive behavior, which might impair the process of analysis. Try to "fix the problem, not the blame." The time to deal with incompetents is during the crisis (replace them) and in the planning and training process. Either train them to competence or put them where they can't do any damage.

The other thing a post-mortem accomplishes is to allow us to vent and express our emotions. One of the most interesting experiences I had while writing this book was the opportunity to interview or debrief participants in major crisis events soon after their occurrence. While I would begin the interview with a carefully prepared list of questions, I invariably ended up listening as the story poured forth in a torrent of thoughts. Some were at first reluctant to talk, but most were carried away by their own need to recount the event once they began. This psychic decompression, the need to release the pent-up emotional pressure, is an important function during crisis resolution. Oftentimes participants are reluctant to speak about events for fear their intense emotions or the gruesome details will shock the listener. In some cases it may be advisable to allow crisis counselors or mental health professionals to assume this role.

It is important that people receive reassurance from others that they did really do their best under the circumstances. You can't allow a crisis to ruin your life or the lives of others. Understand that we are all human and make mistakes. Channel any feelings of guilt into resolve to prepare, train and do better in the next crisis. Always stay focused on the fact that the crisis resolution phase is the same as the pre-crisis phase. A (new) **crisis will occur**. It may be the same crisis, if you haven't dealt with it effectively, or a different crisis. Don't spend too much time feeling relief over the end of the crisis. Begin preparing for the next one.

THE AMTRAK RAIL DISASTER

Let's examine the crisis resolution phase of the Amtrak rail disaster. As we said previously, this was an example of successful crisis management. But why did the collision happen in the first place?

Immediately afterwards, the National Transportation Safety Board (NTSB) began an investigation. The NTSB is mandated by Congress to determine the probable cause of major transportation "accidents". Its findings are subsequently published and are available to the public on request. According to the NTSB report the probable cause of the collision was, "...the failure of the apprentice locomotive engineer to reduce speed in sufficient time to negotiate the curve into Back Bay Station as a result of inadequate supervision provided by the locomotive engineer." In addition, the NTSB faulted Amtrak for failure to provide quality oversight for its engineer training program and for failure to have automatic warning devices for speed reduction ahead of the curve at Back Bay Station. The NTSB made several recommendations to both Amtrak and the Engineers' and Transportation Workers Unions to prevent similar collisions in the future.

The NTSB further concluded that, "The emergency response personnel in Boston reacted promptly and in appropriate numbers to the emergency."

Our own hospital post-event evaluation process revealed that the hospital disaster plan had functioned well. Personnel had been familiar with the elements of the plan and had carried it out appropriately. We used the opportunity to consider additional contingencies. What if a similar disaster had happened at night? Would our staffing be adequate? Was our call list up to date? Could we get additional staff as necessary? On the whole, however, we concluded that all our efforts in terms of planning, preparation, training and running disaster drills had paid off.

I was also at that time a member of the Conference of Boston Teaching Hospitals EMS Committee. This group of doctors and hospital administrators met regularly to coordinate the hospital plans with Boston EMS. The COBTH EMS committee's assessment of the event was likewise positive.

The NTSB report also noted that the Boston Fire Department has an ongoing training program with the MBTA and conducted drills with MBTA personnel to familiarize them with fire safety equipment and facilities. During these drills the fire department inspects the smoke control system and exits. The June 1990 City of Boston Disaster Drill (they are staged at 6-month intervals) had included exercises with mock hazardous materials and extrication of passengers from trains, trolleys and buses.

In my own opinion the heroic performance of the train crews following the collision was in large part due to their excellent training by Amtrak and the MBTA.

The resolution phase of this crisis gratifyingly wound up with commendations from the Mayor's office for all the participating hospitals and agencies as well as thank you letters from Amtrak and the MBTA. The hospital also received a letter from the Amtrak engineer both thanking us for his care and commending us for the way media attention was managed.

UNITED AIRLINES FLIGHT 232

The resolution phase of the crash of United Airlines flight 232 (chapter 6: Preparation and Training) provides us with some potentially valuable, although tragic information. Of the 110 people who died in the crash, autopsies revealed that 35 died from smoke inhalation rather than the actual impact trauma or burns from the fire. Of these, 33 were in one section of the plane in which the roof of the fuselage collapsed, making escape difficult. The solution to the problem of fire suppression in a jet airplane crash has yet to be completely solved.

As a result of technical analysis, an ultrasonic inspection program was designed to verify the airworthiness of the engine fan disks. This was the engine part that failed, severing the hydraulic lines and resulting in the loss of hydraulic powered controls.

Another point during the post-crash analysis was the advisability of infants and children being restrained in appropriate safety seats rather than sitting on a parent's lap.

JOSEPH

The biblical scholars among you will remember the resolution phase of the Joseph story. The famine does indeed occur and Joseph uses the stored grain to save Egypt from starvation. In the process he cements his reputation and the status of his family. They all live "happily ever after" until (of course) a **new crisis occurs** in Exodus, chapter 1.

THE ELEVATOR CRISIS

Let's return now to Chapter 2. Are you wondering what happened in the elevator crisis? Think back. We left our hero in an elevator, accompanied (just to make things more complicated) by his wife and confronted by a gunman. As per the planning and preparation in "plan A" he expeditiously hands over his wallet. He cannot however execute the second critical half of "plan A" (which is to run like hell) because 1) he is in an elevator and 2) his wife is not acquainted with "plan A". He has committed two (potentially) fatal errors:

- Failure to provide for contingencies
- Failure to communicate the plan to the rest of the team

As we could easily predict, according to Murphy's Law, the next words out of the gunman's mouth are, "That's not enough."

Lets analyze the situation. Our hero has no "plan B". He has no significant training in hand to hand combat and the other guy has the gun. His wife is there, so there's another life at risk in addition to his own. What could happen? Murder. Rape. Murder and Rape. Do we have time for problem solving here? Perhaps a decision matrix? I don't think so.

This is what I refer to as an "OH SH-T" experience. Frozen by indecision, in a complex situation with no predetermined plan, the next move is made by the gunman. The elevator door opens and he leaves. Sometimes you just get lucky. The point of this story and of crisis resolution in general, is to learn from your mistakes and the mistakes of others. Based on this knowledge you are better equipped to plan, prepare and train for any similar crisis in the future. Needless to say our hero now has a plan B, which has been communicated to other team members and has involved some considerable training. Trusting to luck is not prudent in a crisis situation. As we have learned in the previous chapters on prevention, preparation and training, we want to do everything possible to tilt the odds in our favor and remain as much in control of a situation as is possible. This will not guarantee future success, but it's the best we can do. More often than not these efforts will pay dividends in the long run.

CRISIS DOCUMENTATION

The last thing most people would think about during a crisis situation is taking notes. After all, in a true crisis when the action is fast and furious, who has time to write down everything that's happening? This is a potentially serious oversight. As we have already seen in our study of crisis resolution, learning from our conduct during the crisis is critical to improved performance in the next crisis. In addition we may find it necessary later on to justify our actions during the crisis in the face of criticism by all the "Monday morning quarterbacks" who use the advantage of "20/20 hindsight" to tell us what we should have done. If that is not sufficient justification, let's introduce the concept that the very act of documentation during the crisis can actually improve real time crisis management.

For suitable examples let us again look at the practice of emergency physicians. The bane of my existence in the ER is "documentation". It often takes me as long, or even longer, to write up a patient's chart as it does to see and treat the patient. Yet I force myself to struggle through, at times spending hours after the end of my shift, dictating charts. Even as I see the patient, take the history and do the physical exam, I make notes. These help me later on, when I dictate the chart, to remember all the important details of the case. In critical life or death situations I make it a point to sit down immediately after stabilizing the patient to dictate the chart, or at least note the salient points of the case. In cardiac arrest cases or trauma codes we actually have a team member whose sole responsibility is to take notes during the code. This person records every detail, including dosages and times of all drugs administered, the patient's vital signs and any response to therapy.

Why is this documentation so important? For one thing it helps me to learn from every case (crisis) I manage. The very act of writing things down is a memory booster that reinforces the knowledge gained in each encounter. In addition, when I reread my note I can usually remember additional details from the case stored in my subconscious that somehow find release when I review the written facts. My written note has helped me on numerous occasions when the management of the case was reviewed or questioned.

Perhaps the most important function of case documentation is the role it plays in actually helping me to manage the patient. This works because I use a series of templates - essentially symptom based checklists - to generate a record for each patient. These checklists are problem based, developed by a panel of experts and available via a computer based dictation system. They encourage the collection of relevant data and often suggest appropriate therapeutic responses in each case. Since I know ahead of time that I am going to have to "write up" every single case after the fact for potential scrutiny and review I try very hard to manage it correctly so that the chart will be acceptable. More than once I have gotten up in the middle of writing up a case to go back to the bedside and take additional history or perform another examination or therapeutic maneuver because I was prompted to do so by the process of documentation.

Does this relate to crisis management in general or is it a specialized situation? I would make the case that record keeping is useful in most, if not all, crisis situations. It is particularly useful to have a written record for review and analysis to aid in your assessment during the crisis. After the crisis is over the written record can serve as a steadfast ally in justifying your actions and preserving the history of what you have done. This can be particularly important in business or other organizational situations. It can also play a role in a purely personal or private crisis however. Often writing down events and potential solutions will aid in your ability to analyze and manage them.

The necessary corollary is that all record keeping may potentially play a role in some future crisis. Every time you write a letter, send an email, take notes in your computer or on a notepad, you are creating a "paper trail" documenting your actions. Take a moment to look back at the various records you leave daily in your wake. Do they reflect well on what you are doing? Would they stand up under the microscope of public scrutiny? How would they appear to your boss, the press, your spouse, your stockholders, the IRS? If they do not look flattering perhaps you should reconsider how you are conducting your business, or your life.

The Enron scandal of 2002 is a classic example of this premise. At the time of Enron's financial collapse reams of documents were shredded by officers of Enron's accounting firm, Arthur Anderson. The very act of document shredding created a presumption of guilt in the mind of the public. Documents which might need to be shredded should never be created. Actions, which may need to be hidden in this manner, should not be taking place.

EXERCISE

Review a recent crisis you have managed or know thoroughly from direct involvement. What was done right? What could have been improved? What preparation or training do you need to better deal with similar situations in the future?

Document the management of this crisis for future reference.

CHAPTER 11

ORGANIZATIONAL SKILLS

Organizational skills relating to crisis management come in two main categories, generic and specific. An example of a specific organizational skill is the development of expertise and/or detailed procedures and techniques (through planning preparation and training) for dealing with a hazardous material spill at a chemical plant. In fact, an entire organization might be built around a series of specific organizational skills designed to deal with crisis situations. A good example of this is a fire department. Another is a hospital emergency department. Specific organizational skills need to be developed on an ad hoc basis in response to the unique requirements of individual situations. They should be recognized as special skills and maintained in accordance with their level of importance. The delineation of specific organizational skills is beyond the scope of this book. Needless to say they require careful development, training and maintenance. This may mean continuing education or retraining and practice at regular intervals to reinforce these skills and prevent any deterioration in performance.

Generic organizational skills are to a large degree the basis upon which specific skills may be built. As such they are of general importance and will be discussed in some detail. They include:

TEAMWORK
LEADERSHIP
FOLLOWERSHIP
COMMUNICATIONS
LOGISTICS
IMPLEMENTATION

TEAMWORK

The definition of teamwork is: "Concerted effort or action by the members of a group to achieve some common end." The key aspect of teamwork is its group nature. For a team to function properly there must be a group ethic, group loyalty and group goals. Each individual team member feels allegiance to the team rather than merely to himself or to any particular individual. Often the team leader commands allegiance and respect as well. Ideally each member of the team brings unique skills and capabilities to the team, which contribute to the groups competence and capacity. Team sports are, of course, the classic example of teamwork in action. In football for instance, it takes the coordinated effort of 11 people, each doing an assigned individualized task, to advance the ball down the field. A cardiac arrest team likewise is composed of multiple individuals, each performing a different task with the common goal of saving a life. Team members may have trained for years together and know each other intimately. On the other hand they may have assembled in an instant and not even know each other by name. The most important factor is how they function as a team. Can they work together effectively to perform the assigned task. Practice is essential to competent team based performance, especially whenever technical skills are involved.

A good example of teamwork in action during a crisis is seen in the previous chapter titled "MAJOR CRISIS". In this instance a team of individuals, the Conference of Boston Teaching Hospitals EMS Committee, crafted a disaster plan for the city that linked the major Boston hospitals (teams) to the city's Emergency Medical Services (team).

Each team in turn designed it's own plan dealing with it's particular responsibilities. The teams then practiced individually and together, during annual citywide disaster drills, to test the plans for flaws, make improvements and familiarize their team members with the elements of the plan.

LEADERSHIP

Leadership is a critical organizational skill. Not everyone sees him or herself as a leader. Yet in times of crisis, when leadership is called for, it may be incumbent upon any of us to assume the mantle of leadership. One of the most dangerous situations in a crisis is the absence of leadership. Although leadership was discussed previously under personal skills (refer back to that section if necessary for review), it is important to recognize it as a key organizational skill as well. Even if you are not the designated leader on the organizational chart circumstances may call you to a leadership role. This is a good example of crisis as opportunity. The organization's crisis is your opportunity to prove yourself in a leadership role. Performance under pressure is a prized organizational skill. It will be remembered long after the crisis has passed.

An example of leadership is the action of Randy Still in Chapter Eight on "Event Management." By taking appropriate action in a crisis he led the rest of the crew to take control of the situation. Often leadership by example is more immediate and effective than simply giving orders.

FOLLOWERSHIP

Although much less romantic and visible than leadership, the ability to be a good follower in times of stress is crucial. Dependability is a valuable quality within any organization. A team member who can be counted on to deliver, especially in time of crisis, is an invaluable member of the team or organization. Before you can be a good leader you need to learn to be a good follower. This will help you later, as a leader, to know what to expect of members of your team and to know what they, in turn, expect of you

COMMUNICATIONS

Without reliable, appropriate communication, crisis management falls apart. You can have the best plan in the world, the best leader, the best followers and the best team. Without good communications, nothing will work as planned. Unless the plan is communicated properly to the entire team, in such a way that its members understand the plan and the importance of their individual roles, the plan will become a fiasco. Each team member must know how his role fits into the plan. Why? So that he grasps its importance relative to the overall plan and understands that the team is counting on him to perform. Also, if for any reason he cannot execute it as planned, the team member must figure out the next best thing to do. At the very least he should communicate this failure immediately to the team leader. There's nothing worse in a crisis than having an error of failed execution compounded by failed reporting.

Communication during a crisis is critically important. Remember, Murphy's Law still applies. When (not if) things start to go wrong and the plan seems to be unraveling the ability to communicate may be all that stands between you and complete disaster. Are your phone lines adequate and secure in an emergency? Do you have a redundant system for back up, such as cell phones? Do key team members have pagers? Who will you need to be in contact with? What are the phone numbers for your team members, leadership, logistical support, affiliated agencies, the media? Do you have a "calling tree" that will facilitate the making of large numbers of calls? Is there a central "command center" number known to all members of the team? Communications planning must take place in advance or your entire plan could fail at the most critical juncture. One of the crucial elements that went right during the Amtrak rail crash (refer back to Chapter 9 titled, "Major Crisis") was the possession by Boston fire rescue personnel of a communications device which allowed mobile communications inside the train tunnel, where ordinary cellular phones and radiophones were useless. A good example for a home based crisis would be easy availability of a wireless phone, which could be used outside the house in case of fire.

It makes sense to appoint a crisis communications team. One of its members should sit on the crisis management team in order to foster (you guessed it) good communications. The team should designate a spokesperson responsible for interfacing with the media. It needs to establish communications policies and protocols. For example, all requests for media interviews should be referred to the spokesperson. The spokesperson and the rest of the team should engage in appropriate planning, preparation and training. The team should identify modes of communication (TV, radio, print media, internet, direct mail) and the various audiences to which it should be directed. These include employees, customers, suppliers, investors, regulators, other "stakeholders" and the general public.

LOGISTICS

Logistics is the discipline that deals with the procurement, maintenance, movement and disposition of equipment, personnel, facilities and supplies. In a crisis situation, where you may be expecting supernormal effort from your team, they have the right to expect some very basic things from you. In addition to the necessities of life, such as food and shelter, they need the equipment necessary to perform their assigned task. They need it at the point of use, in working condition, at the time it is needed. Feeding lunch to three people is no big deal. Feeding lunch to 3000 people is a very big deal. This is the prosaic, "An army marches on its stomach" analysis. Neglecting the logistics implications of any crisis situation puts you and your organization in great peril.

In many crisis situations the participants work with such fervor and dedication that they have to be reminded to take breaks to eat, rest, sleep and recover from their exertions. Failure to account for this will result in crisis fatigue. Failure to provide even the best, most dedicated people with the basics of life and necessary equipment may result in failure to manage the crisis or only limited success.

IMPLEMENTATION

In any situation, whether it is organizational or personal, plans need translation into action. Once the plan is formulated, each aspect of it needs assignment to a specific individual or team that will then be responsible and accountable for its proper execution.

If the plan is well formulated and has been adequately communicated to the individual or team responsible, then you have the best possible chance of success. In addition you must assure that each individual or team has been supplied with the logistical wherewithal to accomplish its task. The team must be well chosen, prepared and trained for that particular task or aspect of the plan. If you have schooled the team in the exigencies of "Murphy's Law" they will be better prepared when things do not go according to plan. Review the section on Murphy's Law and probability to fully understand what you are up against in terms of implementation.

A TEST OF ORGANIZATIONAL SKILLS

On July 17, 1981 an event occurred in Kansas City, Missouri which sorely tested the organizational skills of the Kansas City EMS (emergency medical services) system. At 7:15 PM on a "lazy summer Friday night" in Kansas City, Joseph F. Waeckerle MD was on his way home after finishing a twelve-hour shift in the emergency room. He received an urgent call from EMS dispatch asking him to come to the Hyatt Regency Hotel where the "roof had collapsed." Initially, Dr. Waeckerle replied, "I'm no longer the EMS Medical Director, give him a call." He had recently resigned the post to head up the emergency room group at a suburban hospital. He felt, after eight years, it was someone else's turn to do the job. The dispatcher replied that the Director was needed at the hospital and requested that Dr. Waeckerle come to help with on scene triage. Even after 8 years in the ER, Waeckerle was not completely prepared for what he found.

"The outside of the Hyatt was bedlam. There was a group of more than a hundred injured people on the circular drive in front of the hotel. I walked up to two residents (emergency medicine resident physicians) who were riding the ambulance and asked what I could do to help." They said, "We really need you to take this over."

Waeckerle didn't hesitate for a moment. He began giving orders. His first act was to perform what later came to be known as "geographic triage". By declaring that any of the injured who could walk should move to a designated area he immediately sorted out the seriously wounded from those who were ambulatory.

Next he proceeded inside the Hyatt. If the outside of the Hyatt was bedlam, the inside was "bedlam and chaos combined." The interior of the Hyatt Regency was a huge air-well across which suspended pedestrian bridges or "sky-walks" had been hung.

The bridges were intended as a novel architectural accent and a means to cross from one side of the hotel to the other above the lobby. The fourth floor skywalk had become overloaded with people standing on it during a party. Exceeding its load capacity, the fourth floor bridge collapsed. It landed on top of the second floor bridge. Both skywalks then fell, together, to the lobby below. Hundreds of people had been standing on the two bridges and in the lobby beneath them.

What Waeckerle encountered inside the hotel was shocking. "It was like a war. There was a lot of screaming. Power lines had broken and were swinging above the lobby, arcing electricity. A waterline had ruptured and there were several inches of water on the floor. In it was floating feces and human body parts. You just had to ignore all of it and focus on what you were doing."

Dr. Waeckerle grabbed a bullhorn from the fire department and announced, "I'm Joe Waeckerle and this is what we're going to do." He identified the fire department and police commanders and a command team was formed. Once again utilizing his new technique of "geographic triage", he instructed everyone who could walk (with the exception of the professional rescue teams) to get out of the hotel. "I had to explain to family members looking for loved ones that we could get to them faster if everyone went outside and allowed the rescuers to do their job."

"Then we were able to perform actual triage. I went from person to person, directing resources to each patient." Waeckerle was actually crawling through the wreckage of the fallen skywalks and got stuck several times. "There was a circular staircase that was unstable. They forgot to tell us (until later) that what we were doing wasn't safe."

"A number of people were buried alive. We had to bring in huge cranes to lift the debris in order to get to them." At times the rescuers had to ignore hideously injured corpses, or even dismember them, in their efforts to extricate the living.

Adequate resources were not available to treat everyone at once. "The fatally injured were told they were going to die. This bothered some of the rescuers." These people were mortally injured and trapped. They couldn't be extricated in time. In medicine we're not used to this battlefield concept of triage, that some people are beyond saving and that we need to devote limited resources to those with a chance of survival.

The dying were given pain medication to ease their suffering. "I had to do that for one lady whose family was right in my face, screaming for me to do something. I remember every single time I did it. To this day I pray I did the best I could for each person."

Another man, a bartender, was trapped by his leg. "I told him we had to amputate his leg (to get him out) but he refused. I gave him morphine for the pain. When I came back later on he agreed to the amputation." The man died there in the lobby, as the surgeon worked to free him.

"A lot of people (rescue workers) said, 'I can't do this anymore,' and left. I give them credit for recognizing their own limits and getting out of the way once they could no longer function."

In the final accounting 111 people died at the scene. Only 3 died later, in the hospital. More than 200 were injured, many of them seriously. In the crisis resolution phase there were accolades for the rescuers, who behaved heroically under difficult conditions. Dr. Waeckerle commented, "I won a bunch of awards and was asked to lecture a lot, but I didn't like it. I felt this was all based on the misery and death of a lot of other people."

Later a Jesuit priest pointed out to him that he had been put there for a reason. And that he should share the lessons he had learned with others. "I accepted it after that, but it's still a hard story to retell."

When asked to comment on particular lessons learned and the application of principles of crisis management, Dr. Waeckerle mentioned the following:

LEADERSHIP
"People were looking for a leader and it was relatively easy to assume command." This was facilitated by the fact that Waeckerle was well known in the fire and rescue community and had previously been EMS Director.

TEAMWORK
A "natural command team" was formed, consisting of the medical, fire and police commanders. As each patient was triaged, their definitive care was handed off to a team of rescuers assigned to that patient.

COMMUNICATIONS
"Communications was a problem." The phone lines were out. Portable radios didn't work because of the leaded glass and metal framework of the structure, in addition to all the noise and commotion. Even Waeckerle's bullhorn was eventually shorted

out by water dripping from above. The rescuers had to rely on runners carrying messages by hand to communicate with each other and the outside.

LOGISTICS
Initially there was a shortage of supplies. As the incident progressed fire and rescue squads rapidly provided whatever was needed. Even heavy equipment was brought to the scene in a timely fashion to assist in extrication.

EMOTIONS
"Everyone was overwhelmed (at first) by the scene. The enormity of it, the suffering and death, was very emotional. People (rescuers) were disoriented. They felt crummy. You say to yourself, 'God, what am I doing here?'" Waeckerle says he was later told by a psychiatrist friend, who had served in Vietnam, that in this type of situation, "Seventy five percent of people will be incapacitated and unable to respond." Emotions had to be set aside, even in the face of the most gruesome injuries, in order for the rescuers to function.

"Afterwards it was difficult for a while to be a normal person, a husband and father. I knew I had to talk to someone about it." As a direct result of this event, CID (critical incident debriefing) became an important post crisis requirement in Kansas City and throughout the country.

MEDIA
The police did a good job of containing the media at the scene. There were no reports of interference during the rescue effort. Afterwards there was a "media deluge." Most of the media were pretty fair,

but there were the inevitable critics who, "Had no concept of what happened."

The Hyatt Regency skywalk collapse provided many lessons to the growing specialty area of "Disaster Medicine." Viewed through the lens of crisis management, it continues to be an instructive example.

EXERCISE

Develop a Crisis Management Team at your organization. It needs to be chaired by the CEO or his equivalent and should include key personnel from major areas (communications, public relations, personnel, production, etc.) yet be small enough to be efficient and make quick decisions.

BUSINESS CRISIS

Although this chapter has been titled, "Business Crisis", it contains lessons for non-business organizations and individuals as well.

Let's look at examples of business crisis and see how we may apply the general lessons of crisis management to a specific business crisis.

THE TYLENOL CRISIS

In late September of 1982 a cluster of mysterious deaths involving otherwise healthy people suddenly occurred in the western suburbs of Chicago. A relationship between these deaths was soon established. They were all due to cyanide poisoning. The delivery vehicle of this lethal poison was discovered to be a capsule preparation of the leading non-prescription pain reliever, Tylenol.

The ensuing crisis was unprecedented and, without a doubt, one of the most serious, challenging business crises of all time. Seven people died. The media focused intensely on this dramatic event. Within weeks Tylenol plummeted from its perch as the nation's leading pain reliever with annual sales of close to $450 million, to a product shunned and feared - a total marketing disaster. Market share dropped from 35% to 8%. Some analysts predicted the brand would never recover.

Yet, three months later Tylenol was back on store shelves in new, tamper resistant, packaging. Within 6 months the brand had regained 80% of its previous market share. How was this brilliant and surprising recovery possible? At this point all of you should know the answer—through proper application of the principles and techniques of crisis management.

According to David R. Clare, then president of Johnson and Johnson (JNJ), "There are probably as many emergency plans worked out and ready to go within the Johnson and Johnson organization as there are in any other company that tries to prepare for unforeseen emergencies. But the events surrounding the Tylenol crisis were so atypical we found ourselves improvising every step of the way…. Crisis planning did not see us through this tragedy nearly as much as the sound business management philosophy that is embodied in our credo."

It was this "credo" that served as a decision making tool and guide throughout the crisis. It served as the **generic crisis management plan** or framework, upon which a course of action was formulated. The Johnson and Johnson credo, set forth by Robert Wood Johnson during the 1940's establishes the priority of the company's responsibilities: first to "doctors, nurses and patients", then to "our employees", next to "the communities in which we live and work and to the world community as well. … Our final responsibility is to our stockholders…" (see Appendix 1 for the complete credo).

According to CEO James E. Burke, "Later we realized that no meeting had been called to make the first critical decision - to be open with the press and put the consumer interest first. Every one of us knew what to do. There was no need to meet. We had the credo philosophy to guide us."

It is interesting to note that this credo is more than a typical "mission statement" hung on the wall in the corporate headquarters. Over the years the company has conducted special meetings (**training**) specifically directed towards reinforcing awareness and belief in the credo. Thousands of JNJ employees have attended these meetings and the company feels that the credo permeates corporate decision-making and "forms the bedrock of Johnson and Johnson corporate culture."

What did JNJ do to manage the Tylenol crisis? They gathered as much information as they could as rapidly as possible (**assessment**). They made timely **decisions** based on their credo (**generic crisis plan**). Then they **acted boldly** to implement those decisions.

Johnson and Johnson **pulled out all the stops**. McNeil (the subsidiary that makes Tylenol) employees worked exhausting hours. The company called upon its established relationships with vendors, medical professionals and the public to gain sympathy for its position and cooperation with its recovery effort. Management **focused their attention** and worked intensively and tirelessly to manage the crisis. According to Robert Anderson, a JNJ executive during the crisis, "The chairman put together a 4 or 5 member crisis committee that met at least twice daily.

Sometimes it only met once because the meeting lasted all day."

Johnson and Johnson resolved to **never give up**. Based on information from public surveys, it felt that it was possible to restore the Tylenol brand.

Johnson and Johnson managed: communications, media, people and events.

COMMUNICATIONS

JNJ set up a hotline telephone number. They warned the public of the danger through the news media. They cooperated with federal agencies, including the FDA and the FBI, to both obtain and disseminate information. JNJ communicated internally to its managers and sales people so that they in turn could communicate to retailers and consumers.

Subsequent to the crisis, in the **crisis resolution** stage, the company put together a booklet listing phone numbers of all key personnel which their executives keep with them at all times.

MEDIA

JNJ decided early on to be open and cooperative with the news media. This contributed to a sympathetic stance towards the company by the vast majority of the media. The poisonings after all were not the fault of JNJ. The company was presented by the media as both victim and responsible corporate citizen.

PEOPLE

JNJ surveyed consumers to gather information regarding public perception and how people would likely react to various interventions. Based on this information JNJ resolved to reintroduce the Tylenol brand, moved rapidly to introduce tamper resistant packaging and mounted an aggressive advertising campaign accompanied by discount coupons.

EVENTS

JNJ quickly removed all Tylenol capsule products from the marketplace nationally, even though the poisonings seemed to be local, isolated incidents. Understanding that "perception is reality," they chose to proactively take control of events and book a huge short-term loss in order to gain the long-term goal of maintaining public trust.

In 1986 the Tylenol crisis reappeared like a bad dream. On February 8, 1986 a woman in Westchester County NY died of cyanide poisoning after ingesting extra strength Tylenol. JNJ learned of this on February 10. They immediately got in touch with the FDA and the FBI and dispatched representatives to Yonkers in Westchester County to investigate and act as liaison with the local authorities.

An 800 number consumer "hotline" was established. Three press conferences were held for the media within the first week. On February 11 a limited recall was issued. On February 13 another cyanide-laced bottle of Tylenol was discovered by FDA investigators. An immediate recall of all capsule Tylenol products was issued by JNJ. On February 17 JNJ announced it would change all capsule Tylenol products to a solid, more tamper resistant, caplet form and offered to replace all capsules in the hands of consumers with caplets.

JNJ had learned its lessons well from the **crisis resolution** phase of the 1982 episode. They were able to **manage communication, the media, people and**

events. They employed the successful strategies used in the previous crisis to rapidly resolve the new one.

THE FIRESTONE TIRE CRISIS

The National Highway Traffic Safety Administration (NHTSA) launched an investigation into the question of whether tread separation in certain Firestone tires was occurring at a higher than normal rate and resulting in motor vehicle collisions. A recall of 13 million Firestone tires eventually ensued. According to a Wall Street Journal article, "...The company appeared blind-sided...and made huge tactical blunders..." including blaming customers for poor tire care. The crisis had such serious financial repercussions that it weakened Firestone almost irreparably.

Does this crisis sound familiar? Do you remember when it happened? Do you think it happened in the year 2000? Actually it happened, the first time, in 1978. In fact the events of 1978 are strikingly similar to the current crisis, which began in the year 2000 and continues to this day.

In May of 2000 the National Highway Traffic Safety Administration (NHTSA) launched another investigation into the question of whether tread separation in certain Firestone tires (ATX and Wilderness) was occurring at a higher than normal rate. This similarly caused concern and in fact precipitated a crisis at Ford Motor Company which had installed the tires as original equipment on their Ford Explorer SUVs.

On August 9 (three months later) Firestone announced a voluntary recall stating that, "The safety of consumers is the company's first concern." On September 11 (four months later) Firestone replaced their public relations firm. On October 10 (five months later) Firestone replaced the CEO. On December 19, 2000 (seven months later) Firestone announced the findings of its "...intensive four month analysis..." and instituted "new systems and improvements in the area of quality assurance..." in an effort to "...restore consumer confidence..." Over the course of several months this crisis had a very significant impact on sales at both companies. The collisions cited involved at least 170 deaths (according to NHTSA) and more than 700 injuries. There was tremendous negative impact due to litigation as well as adverse publicity. In late May of 2001 Ford issued a recall of 13 million Firestone Wilderness AT tires. At the same time Jacques Nasser, CEO of Ford, said that he was caught off guard by a letter from Firestone's CEO John Lampe, which formally severed the 95 year relationship between the two companies. In fact, at the time of this writing, the final outcome of this crisis is still unknown.

The 1978 crisis had such serious financial impact that a much weakened Firestone was ultimately acquired by the Bridgestone Company in 1988, continuing to operate as a subsidiary under the Firestone brand name.

Based on the similarity of events, which assume an almost déjà vu character when you read the news reports, Firestone (Bridgestone) did not learn from the 1978 tire recall crisis. They failed to put into place effective practices to **prevent** an identical future crisis. They similarly failed to **plan** or **prepare** for the possibility of a recurrence of such an event. Based on their delayed and at first tentative, response, there is no evidence that their management team was **trained** in **event management**. Firestone repeated many of the same **mistakes** made in the earlier recall.

They initially tried hard to downplay the seriousness and extent of the problem, tried to shift blame onto the consumer and onto Ford for improper tire inflation recommendations. Firestone was slow to react. They took months to ultimately take the steps necessitated by the crisis and **implement** the recall. Even then they were **logistically** unprepared to deal with the large number of tires and customers. They did not appear to do well **managing** the **media**, **relationships**, or anything else until many months after the crisis first appeared.

MULTIPLE CRISES

The final topic to be discussed in this chapter is the concept of multiple crises. These may be sequential, concurrent or both. The fact that I have chosen to discuss it in the chapter on business or organizational crisis does not mean that it cannot happen in an individual crisis situation. In fact, most often, it will involve a combination of personal and organizational crises.

You can relate to the scenario. You're "having a bad day". **Murphy's Law** is in full force. Everything is going wrong. Your car has a flat in the morning and you're late for work. This triggers a confrontation with your boss who's been meaning to talk with you anyway about the project your team is involved with at work. Meanwhile your spouse calls to say you left the garage door open and your golf clubs have been stolen. Your spouse was in the garage because the school called to have a parent pick up your son, who tripped playing basketball and broke his ankle. Your spouse is calling from the emergency room and wants you to come right away.

Has this sort of thing ever happened to you? If it

hasn't, you're a very lucky person. How did you deal with it? Could you have done better? Are these really **crisis** situations? You could certainly classify any of them as a **minor crisis**. They each have the potential of becoming a **major crisis**, depending on how we handle them and on **Murphy's Law.** Cumulatively, they certainly seem to assume the proportions of a **major crisis,** at least to you.

How do you deal with simultaneous, or multiple crisis situations? The answer is one at a time—the same way emergency physicians do. The board-certification examination in emergency medicine is a two-part test, written and oral. As part of the oral examination the candidate is presented with a series of three patients. These are presented sequentially and then managed simultaneously to completion of the exercise.

While technically the examinee is managing three patients at once he is in fact only **focused** on one of the three at any point in time. He deals with each patient in turn, coming back to the others once test results and procedures are completed. Computers are good at managing simultaneous, real-time, operations. Humans are not. It is difficult and dangerous to attempt to manage more than one critical situation at a given point in time. We tend to lose focus, get confused and make mistakes. A good practical example is the increase in auto collisions resulting from cell phone use while driving.

Emergency medicine is a particularly good model for dealing with multiple concurrent and sequential crises. We know for sure that this will happen frequently. Actually it happens just about every day. So much so that it has become a fact of life - just another routine day in the ER. At any given point in time an emergency physician might be managing 3, 4, 5 or more patients at one time, like a juggler with many balls in the air.

How do emergency physicians deal with it? We **triage** patients by priority. We do first things first. We organize into **teams**, often a different one for each patient. We provide our patient care teams with appropriate logistics and support. We **train** for the full spectrum of individual and group crisis (disaster) situations. We **plan**, **prepare** and **practice, practice, practice**.

EXERCISE

Compare and contrast the response to crisis of Johnson and Johnson to that of Firestone. Consider the relative time frames of the two events. How well did each company **assess, decide** and **act**? How well did each do in the realm of **event management** with **communication, emotions, stress, the media, expectations, people and events**? Which organizational skills (or lack thereof) were demonstrated in each case? Think about what you would have done in the Firestone crisis if you were in charge.

EXERCISE

Prepare a crisis simulation exercise for an organization with which you are affiliated. List all the necessary steps as outlined in previous chapters. Consider running through the exercise with the management of the organization.

CHAPTER  13

PERSONAL SKILLS

There are a variety of personal skills, both technical and intellectual, which will stand you in good stead in times of crisis. Some of these skills you doubtless possess already. Others should be developed, cultivated and practiced. The time to do this is NOW, in the pre-crisis phase. At times of crisis there is little opportunity to develop complex or unfamiliar skills. Some of the skills I will discuss are generic and are useful in a wide variety of crisis and non-crisis situations. Others are specific, dealing with narrowly defined, but critical, crisis situations. Mastery of these skills will give you the confidence to deal with innumerable types of crisis. Refer back to the chapter on training to reinforce the concept of skill acquisition.

TECHNICAL SKILLS
FIRST-AID (CPR)
SELF-DEFENSE
SURVIVAL SKILLS
PHYSICAL FITNESS

INTELLECTUAL SKILLS
PROBLEM SOLVING
ATTITUDE
COURAGE
FAITH
LEADERSHIP
NEGOTIATION
MANAGING RELATIONSHIPS

TECHNICAL SKILLS

FIRST AID

I will state unequivocally that every adult and every child over the age of 11, should learn basic first-aid. This may literally save your life, the life of a loved one, an associate or another deserving human being. Many good courses are available on first aid through a variety of agencies. Be sure the course you select includes basic cardiopulmonary resuscitation (CPR).

SELF-DEFENSE

We live in a dangerous world. While it is certainly prudent to avoid obviously dangerous situations, no place is completely safe. Danger may even come from associates at work or family members. Self-defense should be regarded as a basic personal skill. I do not think everyone needs to be an expert in karate or some other martial art. I do believe however, that a good basic self-defense course is a prerequisite for life in modern times. I would suggest a course that teaches physical skills and techniques as well as mental preparedness.

SURVIVAL SKILLS

If your existence revolves around home and work and you would never consider venturing out into the "wilderness" you may feel no need of survival skills. Yet, how many people now travel by air, or even by car, through remote areas? Would you be equipped to cope with a prolonged power outage during cold weather, or a natural disaster such as an earthquake, severe storm, or flood? Millions of Americans do travel to wilderness areas for vacation and recreation. Hiking, skiing and a variety of water sports, to name but a few, could put almost anyone in immediate need of survival skills. Basic survival skills are for everyone. They should include: the ability to swim and float, knowledge and skills in staying warm in the cold, including how to safely build a fire (matches are allowed) and knowing what to do if lost. Survival skills can be acquired through a variety of courses and classes given by organizations such as the YMCA and local health clubs (swimming), scouting programs (for boys and girls) and outdoor training oriented organizations such as Outward Bound.

PHYSICAL FITNESS

It is not hard to imagine a crisis situation in which physical strength or endurance might play a role. It often is difficult, however, to maintain the level of resolve necessary to engage in an exercise routine on a consistent, regular basis. I can tell you that it definitely is worthwhile, for your general health as well as your ability to deal with crisis. A serious exercise regimen is sustainable only if it becomes part of your lifestyle. The goal here is not to develop bulging muscles or run a marathon, but merely be better prepared to deal with the vicissitudes of life. Any adult should consult his physician before undertaking such a program, both regarding his capacity and a suitable regimen of exercise. Remember the goal is to prepare you for crisis, not create one.

INTELLECTUAL SKILLS

The kinds of intellectual skills you need to develop lend themselves less readily to canned courses and training sessions, although courses on some of them, such as leadership and negotiation, are certainly available. These tend to be skills that develop, as in the physical realm, through exercise. Use them regularly and they will be second nature in a crisis. If you depend on summoning them up from the distant past they may be less readily available.

PROBLEM SOLVING
Refer to the previous treatment of this topic in Chapter 7. Catalog and practice it along with your other personal skills.

LEADERSHIP
A good leader projects confidence and has a clear vision or **plan**. He is ethical, leads by example, understands the value of **teamwork**, is able to delegate, encourages his team and can be personally persuasive. Charisma is helpful, but definitely not necessary. Any one can become an effective leader if you try hard enough.

"But be not afraid of greatness: some are born great, some achieve greatness and some have greatness thrust upon 'em." (Shakespeare, Twelfth Night II, 5)

Practice in the leadership role. This is easy in volunteer organizations, or even in business, where often no one wants to step forward to assume leadership (and hence accountability) in a particular undertaking. Also refer to the section on leadership under organizational skills.

NEGOTIATION

Negotiation is an invaluable life skill. Whether you realize it or not you are involved in negotiation every day. You negotiate with your family members, boss, coworkers, subordinates and even strangers on the street. In a crisis situation negotiation skills (or lack of them) are often critical to success or failure. You may need to negotiate to resolve a conflict, to obtain assistance, for time to complete a task, or permission to undertake a specific action or intervention. You may even have to negotiate for life itself. Many good books have been written on negotiation. See the list in References and Resources at the end of the book. Read several of them. Learn this skill and practice it regularly.

ATTITUDE

"The will to survive is the most important factor... If you are not prepared mentally to overcome all obstacles and to expect the worst, the chances of coming out alive are greatly reduced." (Survival, Evasion and Escape, Department of the Army Field Manual). While this statement is made in a book on survival training it relates equally well to all other aspects of crisis management. A can do (or must do) attitude often produces results bordering on the incredible. As a medical student I once asked my intern how it was that he was always able to start an IV, even after I had failed. His response was, "I'm the intern, **I have to.**"

A positive mental attitude comes, to some degree, from confidence, but largely stems from practice. It can be developed through mastery of the other skills mentioned above and their continual application to real-life situations. Try to see the glass as half full, rather than half empty. Look for the opportunity in every situation, no matter how bleak it may at first appear.

Along with this comes the quality of tenacity, the mental toughness to stick with something we believe in against overwhelming odds. A story is told about President Theodore Roosevelt, who had overcome many obstacles in both his political and personal life. He was being interviewed by a reporter in his den, which was filled with the mounted heads of big game animals. "You must be a very good shot." commented the reporter. "No," said Roosevelt. "I'm an average shot, but I shoot a lot." If an event has a one in a million chance of occurring and we try it a million times our probability of success approaches 100%.

COURAGE

One dictionary definition of courage is, "Fearlessness". I strongly disagree with this as a working definition. For the purposes of crisis management we will define courage as, "The ability to overcome fear." Or, similarly, "The ability to act in the face of fear." Why is this an important distinction? There certainly are instances in which people perform acts of bravery and later profess to have had no fear. For the purposes of crisis management it is much more important to be able to function when you are scared witless—to perform rationally and execute a predetermined plan in the face of spine chilling fear. This is important because it is normal to be afraid in a crisis. We need to plan for the rule, not the exception.

How, then do you develop the "personal skill" of **courage**? Quite simply, the same way you are developing all your other skills, through **practice** and **training**. As we said in the chapter on event management (relative to managing fear), start by doing the things you fear. Volunteer to give a speech before an audience. Accept a challenging assignment. Visit someone seriously ill or dying in the hospital. Take a skiing lesson, or a swimming lesson. Choose the things that are particularly fearful to you. Once you have done them you will have overcome that fear. How does that make you feel? Might it be a little easier to do that same thing the next time? Will you be less afraid, more confident of yourself, perhaps both?

Will this help in a real crisis situation where the level of fear is significantly higher than during a skiing lesson? Yes, it will. You have learned a process that can be applied regardless of the degree of fear. You have also gained the confidence of having mastered your fears in the past.

Another helpful technique is desensitization through repetitive exposure to the environmental cues which elicit fear. In the military, for instance, training sometimes takes place using live ammunition to familiarize soldiers with the sights, sounds and smell of battle.

As a medical student I remember observing one day at a cesarean section, a particularly bloody and at times emotional surgical obstetric procedure. I watched intently as the surgeon opened the woman's uterus, from which gushed a large volume of blood and amniotic fluid, followed immediately by a blood-covered, quivering infant. When I turned to make a comment to the student standing next to me he was no longer there. He had fainted and was lying on the floor. That student later went on to become an obstetrician. He just went back and kept observing until it no longer bothered him.

FAITH

The role of religious belief should not be overlooked. When you are totally exhausted, physically, mentally, or emotionally, from the crisis or multiple crises at hand; when you feel the situation is truly hopeless and that you are helpless to affect the outcome, it becomes invaluable to be able to reach inside yourself for the inner strength to pull yourself through. Examples of people calling upon a higher power at times of crisis are too numerous to mention.

I am not trying to convince anyone of the existence of God, or to make a case for any particular religious point of view. I am merely making the observation that those who truly believe have a powerful tool available in times of stress.

I do not suggest you fall to your knees and pray for divine intervention in time of crisis. In spite of a variety of miracle stories I have heard of or read, I seriously doubt the utility of this as an effective real life strategy. What I am suggesting is that at such a time it can be emotionally stabilizing and mentally reinforcing if you can bring yourself to ask God for the strength to persevere.

My basis for this is derived both from personal experience with my own crisis situations and from the reaction of others at times of crisis. The death of a loved one is one example. It can be an emotionally devastating crisis. Breaking the news of a death to the family is the hardest thing a physician has to do. I have observed over many years of medical practice that faith helps people to cope. It can enable them to deal with death and carry on.

On a more scientific note, statistical analyses and studies by the National Institute of Mental Health demonstrate that attendance at religious services on a regular basis has a positive correlation to longevity and a feeling of well being. Likewise it relates to a decreased incidence of depression and suicide. You exclude the tool of **faith** from **crisis management** to your detriment.

BEWARE OF DEPRESSION

A note of caution: It is completely normal to feel hopeless and helpless momentarily in the face of serious crisis. If this feeling persists however, it may prevent you from performing normal functions for a prolonged period of time. If hopelessness occurs in response to what seems to you, or those around you, to be a minor crisis, it may be a sign of clinical depression. In this case you should seek professional medical help to understand and deal with these feelings.

MANAGING RELATIONSHIPS

How good is your support network? In times of stress can you rely on your family, your friends, or your co-workers, to come through for you? Would they encourage you? Would they lend you money? Would they stick with you through hard times, which might occur in a crisis? Could you trust them with your life?

These are difficult questions. You may or may not like the honest answers. It's better to think about it now, in the pre-crisis stage. While it may not be possible to know for sure it certainly won't hurt to cultivate the key relationships in your life. If you treat others with respect and are always ready to help them when they are in need it is more likely you can expect the same treatment. Likewise if someone has been "dumped on" by you repeatedly, don't expect much in the way of help during a crisis. There are people who may not be dependable no matter what. It's better to know that ahead of time and plan accordingly.

Work continually on developing personal skills. They are an important part of the life long learning process. The more different skills you master and the more you practice the ones you already know, the better prepared you will be in any given crisis situation.

A REAL-LIFE EXAMPLE
OF PERSONAL SKILLS

A story demonstrating the value of personal skills comes from Lori Hermesdorf, a police officer and self-defense instructor in Aurora, Illinois. One day Lori received an email from a former student, Sara Teneike*, who had moved to the East Coast shortly after completing a self-defense course. Lori remembered Sara as a rather pretty, petite woman in her mid twenties. She stood about 5 foot three and weighed little more than a hundred pounds. Her chestnut brown hair was cut in a cute bob that made her look even smaller. Sara initially had some difficulty with the concept of touching strangers, let alone hitting them, when she started the course.

A few weeks after completing the classes Sara had moved to Needham, Massachusetts to begin a career with a high-tech firm. In an email to Lori, Sara recounted the following narrative. Excited about her new job, her mind was totally focused on what she was going to do on a certain Monday morning at work. She pulled into the company parking lot at 8 AM and opened the trunk of her car to get out some materials for a presentation she was preparing. Completely engrossed in thought, she forgot one of the cardinal self-defense rules she had been taught: Always be aware of your surroundings.

She never heard the man come up behind her as she bent over into the trunk of her car. A hand clapped over her mouth. A powerful arm squeezed her against him at the waist. He whispered in her ear, "Don't scream."

Instantly the lessons that Lori had drilled into her in the self-defense course took over. Sara began pummeling the attacker's midsection with elbow strikes. Stunned, he loosened his grip. Sara spun around and caught him in the groin with her knee. Her assailant fell to the ground, but Sara only saw him go down out of the corner of her eye as she ran. Abandoning her purse, her papers and her open car, she dashed for the security of her office, just like she had been taught in the class. When she returned later with the police and a company security guard her purse and belongings were still lying on the pavement. Her attacker was nowhere to be found, but Sara was safe, thanks to her **personal skill** in **self-defense** and to **planning**, **preparation** and **training**.

EXERCISE

Make a list of these personal skills on a 3X5 card. Schedule time for training and skill development. Check them off your list as you master them.

EXERCISE

Make a list of those people you think you could count on in a crisis. If the list seems short work on cultivating your relationships.

CHAPTER 14

PERSONAL CRISIS

In light of the previous chapter on personal skills, and mindful of all our other crisis management techniques let's take a look at some personal crisis situations.

Tony Giancarlo* built a successful business from the ground up. After many years of hard work, long hours and considerable anxiety over whether the business would thrive or even survive, he sold his company to a major competitor for a considerable sum. You might think that this hardly merits the label "crisis", but as Tony told the story it was clear that this was a major turning point in his life. For as long as he could remember he had worked hard for long hours. Twelve, 16, or even 24 hour days were not unusual. Suddenly he went from a situation where he was always working to being "retired".

At first he reveled in his newfound freedom. He spent more time with his family and rediscovered hobbies he hadn't indulged in years. Gradually he began to feel that managing his assets was now his "job" and began to trade more actively on the stock market.

Tony also used this time to spend some time with himself and think about what he really wanted to do with the rest of his life. He realized that he had to "work" at something to maintain his intellect and self-esteem.

Initially Tony was doing very well on the stock market. The bull market was in full swing and it seemed as though he had the golden touch. Everything went up.

Interestingly, Tony recognized the euphoric feelings he was having as a danger sign. Previous experience warned him that a sudden change might be imminent. He recognized this warning and took it seriously. He examined his personal financial situation and resolved to do two things. The first was to diversify some of his investments out of the stock market into real estate and bonds. The second was to actively pursue new ventures as a source of future income and "insurance" against financial adversity.

The second resolution was the easier of the two since he had already decided to work for other reasons. The first was very hard. He was doing so well it seemed almost a shame to pull any money at all out of the stock market. What if he could double his investments in the market?

In retrospect, Tony says, he didn't do enough. In January of 2000 the stock market headed down. Every day he would log on to his computer screen and watch more money evaporate, like steam rising from a boiling pot of water. In the beginning it was only the "play money" he had "won" the year before. Soon, however, it began to eat into money he had actually earned. Nothing was working out. The "income stream" from the stock market had reversed course and turned into a huge cash drain.

Tony developed a sick feeling in his stomach each day, as he monitored his account. It began to affect his outlook and demeanor. His wife and friends remarked that they could tell what the stock market was doing on any given day by how he looked. He became despondent.

Gradually, Tony came to the realization that although he had lost an incredible amount of money in a very short period of time he was going to be OK. Because of his **recognition** of a potential **crisis** and advance **planning,** he still had some reserves for the future. Any one of his several new ventures might succeed in helping him back financially. More importantly he still had good health and a supportive family who understood the situation and didn't try to blame him for making a mistake. In the end Tony felt very lucky and was able to move on with his life.

PERSONAL CRISIS #2

(Based on "Patient Number One" © 2000 by David Fisher and Rick Murdock, Crown Publishers, NY)

Richard Murdock was the CEO of CellPro, a Seattle based biotech company. In December of 1995, while shaving, he noticed a large lump on his neck. Several days later he discovered another one in his groin. Being a biologist he recognized these as enlarged lymph nodes, indicative of some sort of infectious or inflammatory process. Being a man and a busy executive (and feeling basically well) he chose to ignore them. His wife, Patty, began to worry however. Once she found out she reminded him continually to see his doctor and eventually, in January 1996, a biopsy was performed.

The biopsy diagnosis was Non Hodgkin's Lymphoma.

Richard was thunderstruck. "I was in total shock. Not me. It was impossible to believe that the CEO of a company dedicated to curing cancer might actually contract the disease." Patty's response was at once both courageous and functional, "This is just another problem we will deal with and get through."

Electing to undergo conventional chemotherapy, Murdock endured the hair loss, nausea and assorted other nasty side effects that in many respects makes the treatment seem worse than the disease. Then in March of 1996 a repeat lymph node biopsy report delivered the "coup de grace".

The pathologist's report classified the cancer as mantle cell lymphoma, a particularly aggressive form of lymphoma - one resistant to conventional chemotherapy.

In Richard's own words, "I began to consider the possibility I might not survive. I was angry, confused, terrified. But I rebounded. I wasn't going to lie down and die."

What happened next is unique in the annals of medical history. Although in the history of science it is not unprecedented to use oneself as a guinea pig in one's own experiment, I cannot recall another case in which the scientist's own life was at stake.

What Richard Murdock and his oncologist, Ollie Press, proposed to do was a stem cell autograft. This involved removing some of the precursor or stem cells responsible for the production of blood (in the bone marrow) from Richard's body and then treating him with what amounted to a lethal dose of chemotherapy. All of the cancer cells would be killed and Richard's bone marrow along with them. The stem cells then would be reinfused, engraft (grow) in Richard's bone marrow and once again produce blood cells. If the cells did not successfully engraft Richard would die. If they were unable to separate out the tumor cells completely before re-infusing the stem cells the lymphoma would recur. The separation step had never been done successfully before in this type of cancer.

It was at this point in the story that serendipity played a role. It just so happened that CellPro was already working on the necessary cell separation technology. It had been used to separate breast cancer cells, but never for lymphoma.

A team was assembled at CellPro. Over the course of the next three months they developed a process that under normal conditions might have taken years. By the time Richard Murdock went into the hospital for his stem cell transplant on June 17, the cell purification technology had been perfected.

The very fact that I was interviewing Richard Murdock some 5 years after the events described above is testimony to the success of his crisis management techniques.

He told me that although the company (and he personally) had never had a "crisis management plan" per se, CellPro did have a well-defined project development process. "This served as a framework", he said. "We just plugged the problem into the framework."

When I asked him for personal lessons learned from this experience he cited the following:

"When you've been to hell, nothing else looks so bad."

"If I went through that I can go through anything."

"Throw as much (resources) at a problem early on as you can."

"Bring the best minds you can to bear. Get together a good, motivated team and give them room to work."

I particularly liked Patty Murdoch's comment, "This is just another problem we will deal with and get through."

EXERCISE

Reflect back on the lessons you learned in the chapter on "Event Management".

- Assessment, decision, action.
- Pull out the stops.
- Focus your attention.
- Never give up.

How were these factors pivotal in the personal crisis of Richard Murdoch?

EXERCISE

What lessons are there to be learned from Tony Giancarlo's* crisis of euphoria? Remember crisis may be a positive change as well. What elements played a role here? **Planning, crisis prediction, crisis recognition, management of emotions, management of mistakes**. Are there any others you can think of?

CHAPTER 15

SUICIDE

The blue compact car burst through the guardrail and dove nose first, sixty feet down in a graceful arc, into the sea. It landed on a huge boulder in the surf, squarely on its front end, crumpling like a tin can. An explosion blinded the driver on takeoff followed by the earsplitting crash of landing. He had seen and heard nothing he could remember. Slowly consciousness returned and, despite traumatic confusion, he became aware of his situation. He was still alive. He had failed. He couldn't even kill himself.

Paramedics extricated him from the car and brought him to the emergency room where he was evaluated and admitted to the hospital, essentially uninjured, for suicide precautions. We marveled over the crash. The airbag had saved his life in what seemed like a miracle. Yet the story was disturbing. Why should an otherwise healthy 19 year-old boy, with his whole life ahead of him, make such a desperate attempt to end it?

Suicide has been with us since the dawn of recorded history. Socrates drank hemlock rather than suffer banishment from his beloved Athens. The defenders of the fortress Masada slit each other's throats rather than submit to Roman captivity. It has been romanticized in literature (Romeo and Juliet) and even regarded as a badge of honor in wartime by the Japanese Kamikazes. In the United States in our own time it is the 8th leading cause of death overall and the 3rd leading cause of death (after injury and homicide) for people between the ages of 15 and 34. It was declared an epidemic by Surgeon General Dr. James Sacher during the Clinton administration.

In my own personal and professional experience suicide is neither romantic nor heroic. It has always seemed tragic and sad. It often ends life well before it's appointed time and is devastating to the surviving family and friends. Suicide can cast a pall over an entire community. For every successful suicide there are approximately ten unsuccessful attempts, which oftentimes leave the victims crippled, scarred and stigmatized. The youngest suicide victim I have personally seen was 6 years old. It was heartbreaking even to the normally stoic staff of the emergency room.

Often it seems that suicide occurs as the result of some personal crisis - loss of a loved one, the end of a marriage or romantic relationship, a serious financial reverse, illness or disability. Yet crisis is a universal experience. Why do most people carry on and survive the crisis while some choose to end their own lives?

According to a National Institutes of Mental Health panel (1995) there are several risk factors which predispose a person to suicide. These include: familial factors (such as family dysfunction, mental health or substance abuse disorders, or family history of suicide), male gender, a prior suicide attempt, the availability of firearms and exposure to suicidal behavior (by family, peers, or even in the media). Almost all suicides (greater than 90% according to several studies in the medical literature) have a diagnosable mental health or substance abuse disorder. Most have more than one. Before you heave a huge sigh of relief (after all **you** are not crazy or a drug addict) digest these facts: Some 60% of people experience a clinically significant depression at some point in their lives. Anti-depressants are among the most widely prescribed medications, generating billions of dollars a year in sales. Ten percent of the population are alcoholics and an even larger proportion are "social drinkers," not to mention the millions who use "recreational drugs". Even if you personally are not at risk, someone you know, love, or work alongside probably is.

Suicide is an all too common result of crisis. It often seems senseless and without explanation. If we take the time to learn the facts, however, we can discover the risk factors responsible. Vincent Foster, Deputy White House Counsel, shot himself to death in a Washington DC park in 1994. He was suffering from depression and had access to a pistol.

Margaux Hemingway committed suicide by overdosing on sedatives in 1996. The actress was the fifth person in her family to commit suicide. Her grandfather, the famous author Ernest Hemingway, had killed himself with a shotgun 35 years before. He was known to suffer from depression and drink heavily. His father, sister and brother all also committed suicide.

What can we do then to prevent a crisis from resulting in the tragedy of suicide? Thinking back to the chapter on prevention, we can work to **modify risk factors**. By **decreasing risk** and **uncertainty** we influence the odds in our favor. The first step is **recognition**. Consider the possibility of suicide in any crisis situation. Be aware that the combination of adverse life events and risk factors may lead to suicide. Suicide is not the normal response to stress. It may, however, appear as a reasonable response to a person who is confused, irrational, depressed, intoxicated, or in severe distress (either physical or emotional).

Once, during my medical training a middle-aged patient begged me to end her life. She was in severe physical distress from a bowel obstruction and said she would rather die than continue to endure the pain. I sat down with her and explained that I would gladly adjust her pain medication and keep her as comfortable as possible until her obstruction cleared. This was, I told her, a temporary problem that would respond to therapy. Afterwards she could go home to her family and her life (which she ultimately did).

This sort of scenario turns out to be a common precursor to suicide according to mental health authorities. People under stress may experience intense, overwhelming feelings of pain or despair. Confusion or emotional distress blinds them to alternatives. They see suicide as the only solution. This is much more likely in the presence of risk factors.

If you have assessed the risk of suicide and decided you must act, what can you do? The first step is to listen to the other person, empathize and offer support. If the person at risk is yourself, seek out a medical professional (or failing that, a friend) who can perform this role. Be explicit, "I'm considering suicide." They may not guess it based on hints.

Discuss with the person their reasons for feeling hopeless. Offer alternative solutions. Encourage problem solving and plant the seeds of hope. Try to get across the message that the crisis is only temporary. The pain can be survived. Wounds will heal with time. Suicide is permanent. Death is forever. Above all arrange for timely, even immediate, professional help. Don't be afraid to use the word "suicide". You are not introducing thoughts the person has not already had. Ask if they have a specific plan. If so the situation is particularly dangerous. Do not be afraid to call 911 if suicide appears imminent. You would not hesitate in a heart attack. Suicide is every bit as deadly.

Utilize the lessons you have learned to manage crisis: **Assessment, Decision, Action**. Work to modify risk factors. Encourage people with mental health and substance abuse disorders to seek professional help. Depression, substance abuse and many other mental disorders are treatable physiological diseases. In many respects they are no different than diabetes or hypertension. Keep firearms inaccessible to those at risk or to anyone not needing them for a legitimate purpose. Don't be afraid to discuss suicide or to ask seemingly difficult questions. Decrease risk and uncertainty to obtain a more positive outcome. You may save a life.

The blue compact car dove nose first 60 feet down into the sea.

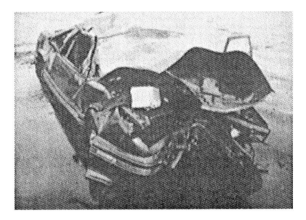

The car landed squarely on its front end and
crumpled like a tin can.

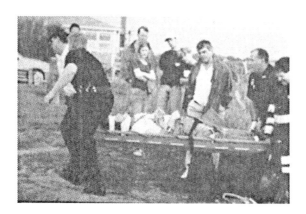

Paramedics extricated the boy from the car.

The airbag saved his life.

CHAPTER 16

CHRONIC CRISIS

When a crisis becomes chronic it ceases to be a crisis. The term "chronic crisis" is an oxymoron, a contradiction in terms. By definition crisis is a "turning point", a "sudden change". How can something chronic be sudden? How long can a turning point go on turning? How then do we label an event, which began as an acute crisis, but then persists into a prolonged or chronic situation? It is now the new status quo, the new reality.

Are we indulging in an exercise in semantics or is there some reason to make this distinction? The reason relates directly to our level of response in a crisis situation. Remember, in a major crisis we want to pull out all the stops, focus our undivided attention and energy on responding to the crisis. Can we really do this if the crisis drags on for weeks or months? It may be challenging to exert this increased level of effort for even a few days (or even hours or minutes of the highest intensity response). Afterwards we need time to rest and "recharge our batteries" before the next episode of supreme effort.

Failure to provide for this is a major mistake in crisis management. A leader can reasonably ask for a supreme effort on occasion, in a crisis situation, but not every day. He certainly cannot ask for it day in and day out for an extended period of time. Doing so will result in "burn out" or what we shall term **crisis fatigue**. In war this is known as battle fatigue. In non-military situations it can result in the practical equivalent of desertion (high turnover), refusal to follow the leader's specific directives, or even mutiny (an attempt to usurp the leader's authority).

A good example of this comes directly from my own experience in the emergency room. While the daily management of multiple medical crisis situations is a major part of the emergency physician's job description, these are by and large each perceived by the physician as a patient crisis and become fairly routine in nature. They become routine through both training and repetition.

If however, too many of these patient crises present themselves all at once they can produce a crisis for the physician, the emergency room and even the whole hospital. All emergency rooms have a disaster plan to deal with the "train wreck" multiple casualty incident. But you can't activate the disaster plan every busy Saturday night. The kind of frenetic activity we so enjoy watching on TV doctor shows about the ER is simply unsustainable by any individual or group over long periods of time. Asking this kind of effort on a routine basis will result in burnout of physicians, nurses and other ER staff. It is also dangerous to patients and staff alike.

Typically what is done is to match staffing levels to patient volume as closely as possible based on historical data. Then "backup" can be arranged to bring in additional nurses and physicians should volumes increase beyond capacity. Where this occurs working conditions are considered good and staffing is steady. Where it does not, retention of staff is difficult. The key to dealing with this situation is that unpredictability of volume is the normal situation in the emergency room, not a "chronic crisis".

Life must go on as usual. People must eat and sleep adequately, attend to their individual business and private concerns. You cannot ask people to operate in crisis mode indefinitely. It simply will not work. Adjust to the new situation as necessary, but adjust.

Another excellent example of what might be deemed a "chronic crisis" is the HIV / AIDS pandemic. This could certainly be classified as a global catastrophe, an ongoing plague, or an infectious disease disaster. To call it a crisis ignores the fact that it has been going on for some 20 years. HIV at present is an ongoing global epidemic, similar to tuberculosis or malaria. Having said that, there are certainly periods and events within the HIV story that would qualify as crisis situations according to our definition of crisis as an "acute turning point". The first reports of the disease in 1981 could certainly be deemed a crisis. Although at first society reacted with an attitude of collective denial, HIV caused a dramatic change in the way we view the consequences of the "sexual revolution."

The effect on the system of blood banking in the United States and other developed countries was a crisis that ultimately caused major changes in the way the blood banks operated. In fact western medicine in general underwent major changes, adopting a system of "universal precautions " that was mainly attributable to the risk of HIV transmission. This could truly be termed a crisis. The discovery of the first effective drug treatment (AZT) in 1987 and then combination therapy in the early 1990's could be termed a crisis in a good sense.

An HIV related crisis is occurring right now in parts of Africa and elsewhere in the developing world where infection rates of up to 25 or even 33% in certain geographic areas threaten to depopulate and destabilize whole countries and wipe out an entire generation. In some of these regions the scale of this plague is of the same magnitude as the Black Death (bubonic plague) of the middle ages. As of December 31, 2000, 21.8 million Africans, including 4.3 million children, have died of HIV and related diseases. In the year 2000 alone, 2.4 million Africans died of HIV and another 3.8 million became infected. One region in Zimbabwe reported a 10% decrease in economic activity solely due to the time people had to spend attending funerals. It is now projected that the average HIV related mortality rate for 15 year-olds in South Africa will approach 50% barring any major new developments. The scale of this plague is staggering—beyond your worst nightmare. It is depressing to even read the statistics.

The next major crisis in the HIV story must be the development of a vaccine. The world will then be challenged with the task of implementing vaccination of a large proportion of the global population.

How has mankind dealt with HIV over the past two decades? Africa and many third world countries have not coped well at all. They have done the equivalent of burying their heads in the sand, failing to **recognize** the very existence of a crisis. There was a failure on the part of many political leaders to react appropriately to **predictions** regarding the future extent of the epidemic. No significant attempts were made at **prevention**. No **planning** took place, without which, of course, there could be no **preparation** or **training**.

In the developed world we have coped somewhat better by eventually adopting the **long-term view** that this is a disease which needs to be constantly battled like heart disease, cancer, malaria or smallpox—through research, treatment and **prevention**. The medical establishment has coped by adopting universal medical precautions, by reforming the blood banking system, by preparing to treat infected people and training healthcare workers in a new set of skills. We have coped by recognizing the HIV epidemic as a **new reality** and **adjusting** - not by treating it as a **chronic crisis**.

Additional examples of what others might be term chronic crisis are long term illnesses (such as diabetes or heart disease), divorce, a family move, or a major financial setback.

In order to cope we must avoid crisis-fatigue, adjust to the new reality and adopt a long- term view.

EXERCISE

Think about a problem in your personal or organizational life that is chronic or ongoing. How have you dealt with it in the past? How might you cope with it better in the future? Have you adapted to it as part of your own new reality? Do you have a long-term plan?

,

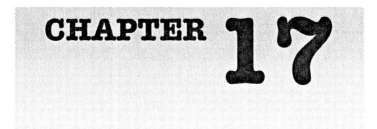

CHAPTER 17

AMERICA UNDER ATTACK

On September 11, 2001 a crisis of unprecedented proportions unfolded before the very eyes of America. Shortly before 9 a.m. eastern time a commercial airliner crashed into the World Trade Center's north tower in New York City. This was followed 18 minutes later by a second crash into the adjacent tower and then by a similar air attack on the Pentagon in Washington DC.

Television audiences watched in horror as two of the tallest buildings in the world collapsed into rubble. The number of people trapped inside, potentially in the tens of thousands, was unknown.

The fact that these were terrorist attacks rather than some horrible accident became grimly apparent with the second crash. All across America air traffic was grounded. Every flight in progress was ordered to land immediately. Evacuations were ordered of many government agencies and large buildings in both cities.

Comparisons to the December 7, 1941 attack on Pearl Harbor were on the lips of news commentators and in the minds of Americans. What would happen next? Will there be a war? If so, against whom?

Alan Friedman was in the Western Union Building on Hudson Street in lower Manhattan 10 blocks north of the World Trade Center at the time of the attack. Suddenly he heard a loud bang. "Someone said a bomb went off in the World Trade Center. Everyone went to the south windows to see what happened. There was a huge hole in the side of the building and a large fire. We all watched in horror, helpless, as people leaped from the roof and the windows of the tower. There must have been a hundred people who jumped."

The north tower of the World Trade Center had been hit by a jet airplane at 8:45 a.m. An enormous hole in the side of the tower was spewing dense black smoke into a blue sky. Suddenly, a second big jet disappeared into the south side of the other tower. Seconds later a huge orange fireball blew out through the north wall. The force of the explosion at the point of impact literally, "Knocked people out of their shoes," if it didn't kill them instantly. Inside the World Trade Center Towers burning liquid ran down the walls. Some exit doors were melted shut by the heat. The very walls of the building itself were cracking. As fires burned on the upper floors, the explosion injected jet fuel and hot gases down the elevator shafts. In the ground floor lobby the elevator doors burst open spewing out blood and parts of human beings. Some of those standing in the lobby were covered with other people's blood. Underground, secondary liquid natural gas explosions were set off, undermining surrounding buildings that collapsed later in the day.

Four hundred New York fire fighters rushed into the two buildings to evacuate people and fight the fires. Accounts from people descending the stairs indicate that the evacuation was orderly. Although some said there was a sense of, "Every man for himself," there is no evidence of a general panic or reports of people being trampled or crushed by the crowd. People bumped into the walls as the building swayed, "Wagging like a dog's tail." Women took off their high-heeled shoes and walked down barefoot. As the office workers made their way down, fireman were struggling up eighty flights along the inner edge of the stairwell. Each man was lugging equipment that appeared to weigh 60 to 80 pounds.

Then at 9:50 a.m., not quite an hour after the second crash, the unthinkable happened. The south tower collapsed. The initial blast blew the fireproof insulation off the tower's structural steel. It was then super-heated above its melting point of 1500 degrees Fahrenheit by 14,000 gallons of burning kerosene jet fuel. The steel bent like wet spaghetti. Once melted, the framework supporting the topmost floors failed. The collapse started from the roof and accelerated as it dropped down in a jackhammer effect, the weight increasing by millions of pounds floor by floor. Each concrete floor deck pancaked into the one below, throwing up a cloud of thick, gray-black dust that resembled a volcanic eruption.

A shower of debris rained down on the streets below. People fleeing the building were crushed by falling concrete, hit by airplane parts and burned by flaming jet fuel. Steel I-beams speared into the ground like arrows, penetrating the three foot concrete liner of the subway tunnel, passing through and embedding themselves deep in the earth beyond.

Minutes later, the north tower collapsed in the same reverse volcanic descent. Fifty thousand people populated the World Trade Center on an average workday. An unknown number were still in the towers when the collapse occurred. Two hundred firemen were initially missing in the collapse and presumed dead, including the Chief of the New York City Fire Department. Rudolph Giuliani, the Mayor of New York, had been in the World Trade Center for a morning meeting. He had just left the towers ten minutes before the attack. New Yorkers ran, panic stricken, away from the imploding buildings, dodging a rain of dust and debris.

Eyewitnesses who heard the collapse described it as a massive shattering sound of glass breaking. The impact of 110 concrete floor decks falling to earth at once (500,000 tons at 120 miles per hour) could be felt all over lower Manhattan as the ground and surrounding buildings shook. The tremor was actually detectable on earthquake measuring instruments as a 2 on the Richter scale. People were streaming north away from the blast zone. A cloud of thick dust thirty stories high, "Like a blizzard, like a snowstorm.", advanced across lower Manhattan. People were frightened. "We thought they were bombing all of lower Manhattan."

The subways were shut down. All bridges into Manhattan were closed to non-emergency vehicular traffic. Major southbound arteries were closed as well. Half the TV stations in New York City went off the air and cell phone service was jammed. The southern tip of Manhattan was described as, "Utter chaos." More than ten thousand people walked across the Brooklyn Bridge trying to escape the carnage.

At 8:40 a.m. American Airlines flight 77, a Boeing

757 jet with 58 passengers and a crew of 6, flew into the Pentagon in Washington DC. The attack left a huge gaping gouge in one of the building's five sides and a persistent fire in its wake. Following this, another commercial jetliner crashed near Pittsburgh Pennsylvania under what at first seemed mysterious circumstances.

One television reporter interviewed a doctor on the scene in New York. Asked what he was doing, the doctor replied he was waiting for patients needing treatment to be brought to him. There were no patients to be seen. Another doctor, interviewed in front of nearby St. Vincent's hospital, which had received several hundred casualties, was asked by a commentator why there weren't more casualties at the hospitals. His face displayed a pained expression. "I think," he said, "And this is a very tragic and terrible thing to say, that most of the casualties are dead."

Two hundred sixty-six people were aboard the four jetliners that crashed. There were no survivors. As of September 13, 2001, three hundred firemen and 60 policemen were missing and presumed dead. Early estimates of the dead at the Pentagon ranged from 100 all the way up to 800 people. Untold thousands were inside the World Trade Center at the time of its collapse. Only time will tell the true toll. We may never know the total for sure. On December 7, 1941 more than 2400 people, mostly sailors and soldiers, died in the Japanese attack on Pearl Harbor. More than 1200 were wounded. Six battleships, three destroyers and seven other ships were sunk. More than half the military planes on the Island of Oahu were destroyed. In terms of the sheer number of lives lost, the terrorist air attack of September 11, 2001 was worse.

As tragic and horrible as this day was, there were positive aspects. In one of the great miracles of modern engineering, the World Trade Center Towers withstood the initial impacts of two 767 jets for 105 minutes (north tower) and 47 minutes (south tower) respectively. This grace period allowed the evacuation of the vast majority of occupants of both buildings prior to their collapse. When the towers finally did fail they rode their corner columns down vertically, in ramrod straight fashion, sparing surrounding buildings and people. According to Jon Magnusson, a structural engineer interviewed by ABC news on September 12, "Ninety nine percent of buildings would have failed immediately. This building stood for an hour. Thousands of people are alive today because the structure took the initial impact and did not collapse immediately." Evacuation stairwells were adequate to allow the majority of the buildings' occupants to escape in time. The engineers and architects of these buildings are heroes who deserve the thanks of thousands for their lives.

New York City's emergency services personnel rapidly moved into action. Police and firemen performed heroically and many gave their lives, in the effort to evacuate the towers. Triage stations for the injured were established on the scene and lines of ambulances soon formed to transport casualties to area hospitals.

As the crisis continued, Americans began searching for answers. How and why did this tragedy occur? What can we do about it? By the thousands people lined up to donate blood. Large numbers of physicians and other health care workers volunteered their services and asked how they could help. Firefighters and rescue workers drove to New York from cities as far away as Chicago, to aid in the rescue effort. New Yorkers vowed to carry on.

But really, what can any of us do? As painful as it may be, in the face of an all too real, very tragic crisis, we must look back to basic principles and try to apply the lessons we have learned. No one has any difficulty recognizing this as a **major crisis.** All the hallmarks are present: **change, conflict, decision, consequences, uncertainty** and **fear.**

Could this crisis have been **predicted?** It was certainly foreshadowed by the previous bomb attack on the World Trade Center in 1993. Didn't our intelligence services know that the twin towers and the Pentagon were terrorist targets? I'm sure they did. I'm also pretty sure they were not suspecting this particular type of attack. It is very difficult to predict an event that has never happened before.

Could the attack have been **prevented?** I suspect strongly that many terrorist attacks have been prevented in the past through vigilance on the part of American intelligence and law enforcement agencies. To quote Madeline Albright, former Secretary of State, "You never hear about what doesn't happen." These particular terrorists are very persistent, however. They just kept trying until they hit on a strategy that worked. At this point in time it is by far more useful to fix the problem than to try to fix the blame.

Can Americans **prevent** a terrorist disaster of this magnitude from happening again? I think it is possible. I will explain how as this analysis proceeds.

What is the assessment of our record in **event management?** How well did we actually deal with this crisis as it occurred? In reference to the emergency response in New York, I think it was handled as well as could be expected under the circumstances. Bystanders in New York described the emergency response as "phenomenal". Police, fire and rescue personnel were immediately on the scene. Although personal transportation was difficult, highway closings facilitated rapid access by emergency vehicles. Traffic in Washington DC on the other hand was described as "grid-locked". The evacuation aspects of crisis management still need work.

In regard to the individual crisis situations on the four airplanes, interesting information is emerging. We must recognize that this incident was very different from our previous experience with airline hijackings. In the past hijackers had usually treated the planes and passengers as hostages. Conventional wisdom had always been, "Submit, cooperate with the hijackers initially. Once they land the plane we can **negotiate** with them based on their demands. If we do have to assault the plane at least it will be on the ground. Above all, avoid doing anything that might cause the plane to crash or result in any loss of life whatsoever." This had usually worked when dealing with refugees seeking asylum, mentally ill people desiring attention or even terrorists seeking recognition for a cause. Coupled with this is the fact that the security measures in force at domestic airports prior to September 11, 2001 had prevented a serious hijacking incident for over 10 years.

The advisability of this stance has changed suddenly and dramatically. It obviously is not going to work against determined, suicidal terrorists, whose main objective is to use the airplane as a flying bomb against secondary targets. The passengers and now even the pilot, are liabilities. They are only in the way. Did the passengers on board the four airplanes know this?

On September 13, ABC News reported a series of conversations that took place by cell phone between Tom Burnett, a passenger on United Airlines Flight 93 and his wife, Deena. The flight had taken off from Newark Airport in New Jersey at 7:01 a.m., bound for San Francisco. The plane carried 38 passengers and a crew of 7, including two pilots. According to reports the plane was hijacked by four men with knives who also threatened that they had a bomb. By the time Burnett called from the plane, events in New York and Washington were all over the news and Deena related them to him. During his final cell phone call, Tom told his wife, "We are going to run this plane into the ground.... We are not going to give up." Deena later said she thought Tom, "... had every intention of **solving the problem**... he was **gathering information** and **coming up with a plan**."

Tom Burnett along with Jeremy Glick, Todd Beamer, several other passengers and possibly United Airlines captain Jason Dahl, apparently did assault the hijackers. Moments later United Flight 93 crashed into a field in Pennsylvania. The passengers and crew of that plane are all heroes who frustrated the hijackers' plan and saved countless other lives. They utilized the three critical elements of event management: **assessment, decision, action**.

CRISIS RESOLUTION

The paradigm has changed. We are now all soldiers in a war not of our choosing. We must **plan, prepare and train**, all of us. We must learn the personal skills of **self-defense**, in order to be **prepared** to resist. The hijackers specifically looked for flights with the fewest number of passengers. They did not relish a fight against even unarmed passengers at odds of 50 or more to one. The Federal Government should consider the use of armed sky marshals on flights. It certainly could immediately arm flight crews with such weapons as pepper spray, batons, stun guns, or non-penetrating firearms. Secure locks and impenetrable cockpit doors are a no-brainer. I have heard security experts in the media decry this approach, saying we cannot turn pilots into policeman. What is the alternative? There is no such thing as 100% security. We cannot keep someone from boarding a plane with a piece of plastic or a razor blade that can be used as a weapon. How do you prevent anyone from saying the cardboard box they hold in their hand contains a bomb? We will not be entirely safe against this form of terrorism until the terrorists know of a certainty that the flight crew is armed, **prepared and trained** and that large numbers of passengers will effectively resist.

If we prevent future hijackings will this stop terrorism? The answer is no. We are involved in a war. President Bush has said it. It is different than any war we have fought before. Wars seem to have a way of changing the rules on us each time around. It is a war of terror, a war against civilians, a war against our freedom. Can't we carry the battle to the enemy, to engage him on his own ground? This is what we hope our Federal Government can do, through appropriate intelligence and action by the armed forces.

We need, however, to first be certain exactly who the enemy is lest we go out precipitously and make a thousand new enemies for every one we have already. This is the province of the executive branch and the military. As Americans we all hope and pray they do the job effectively and quickly, based on the principles of event management: **assessment, decision, action**.

What can we do as individual Americans? First and foremost we must support the government over the long haul. US involvement in World War II lasted five years. The cold war lasted 50. We must make the commitment to sustain an effort lasting many years, if not decades, in order to defeat this foe. We must not underestimate our enemy. These terrorists are desperate and determined. They have taken many years to build up their network of underground cells. To call them cowards, as many have, runs the risk of underestimating the full measure of their danger to our society. While on the one hand we think of attacks on defenseless civilians as cowardly acts, let us not fail to appreciate the resolve of men who **planned, prepared and trained** many months for an action they knew full well would mean their certain death.

The Federal Government has been trying to put its hands on Osama bin Laden since the US embassy bombings in Africa in 1998. What makes anyone think his capture will suddenly be effected? Even if we do find him, there are doubtless others ready and willing to take leadership roles in his place.

America must treat this as a military action, not a criminal or police matter. Had the first World Trade Center Bombing, in 1993, been regarded as an "act of war", we might not be dealing with this new crisis now. America must do more than simply round up the immediate culprits and process them through the criminal justice system. We must find their leaders and as many of their confederates as possible, along with the governments that support them and deliver swift and terrible retribution. Individuals supporting or perpetrating acts of terror in this country should be tried by military tribunals, as would any spy in time of war.

We must enlist the aid of our allies and seek their council. The British, Germans and Israelis, among others, have long experience dealing with acts of terror. We must profit from their successes and learn from their mistakes, as well as our own.

We must endeavor to understand the goals of our enemies. When the Japanese attacked Pearl Harbor in 1941, in addition to crippling US military resources in the Pacific, their main goal was to demoralize America and depress us into a defensive, reactive mode. Instead it had the opposite effect. It galvanized the country into action and solidified our resolve to persevere until ultimate victory. The main goal of this terrorism is exactly the same as that of World War II Japan. They wish to throw us into confusion and despair, to paralyze us with fear, disrupt our economy and our everyday lives. Their hope is to destroy our determination and prevent an effective response.

We must be smarter, more sophisticated and more persistent than the enemy. We must work hard to frustrate their goals and to set and achieve our own. We can win this fight just as we have met serious challenges in the past. Americans have demonstrated this time and again. If we persevere, we will prevail.

WHAT YOU CAN DO NOW

NOW is the time for all Americans to come to the aid of their country. American flags are sprouting like spring flowers all over this country. But patriotic spirit alone is not enough to make a difference. **Plan, prepare** and **train**. Master **personal** and **organizational skills**. Be observant of people and events around you. **ASSESS, DECIDE, ACT**!

SUGGESTIONS FOR SPECIFIC ACTION

Master relevant **personal skills**. Take a course in first aid, self-defense, or a similar subject. Review or draw up your home and personal **crisis plans**.

Donate blood in six weeks and again in six months. Become a regular blood donor. The immediate response has been overwhelming. However, blood can only be saved for about 45 days before it deteriorates. The need will be ongoing.

Volunteer your time in the local community. The initial volunteer response to this disaster must be maintained to meet the ongoing needs of a prolonged struggle.

Contact disaster relief agencies (see the resources section at the end of this book) for local contacts. There is a network of free clinics throughout the United States that would welcome new volunteer physicians, nurses and others.

Host a member of our armed forces for the holidays. In Chicago, the Great Lakes Naval Training Center runs an "Adopt a Sailor" program. Similar programs may be in place near other military bases.

Think about what you personally would do in a terrorist situation. Are you mentally and physically prepared to resist? Are you suitably trained? Are you prepared to be a **leader** or an effective **follower**? Formulate generic and specific plans. Get appropriate training if necessary.

Join or form a neighborhood watch group. Report suspicious activity immediately to the proper authorities (see phone numbers in resources section at the end of the book). Understand the full power of communications, including the internet, cellular phones, television and other media. Get involved. If America develops a hundred million eyes and ears, there will be quite literally no place to hide, for terrorists or any other criminal element. Beware of vigilante action and paranoia. Use your **judgment**. If we overwhelm police and federal authorities with false or frivolous reports we will impair their ability to respond rather than augment it.

Work even harder at your job. One of the main aims of the terrorists is to weaken America by disrupting the economy. We must all labor harder than ever to generate the resources to support the war effort and maintain a free and democratic society. Play a role in assuring that your business and any organizations you belong to have an appropriate **crisis plan**.

Try hard to travel, buy what you feel you need and live a normal life. Be prudent and careful, but avoid the paralysis of fear.

Work to **decrease risk** and **mitigate injury** in your everyday life. Buckle your seat belt every time you drive. Reduce your controllable **risk factors** for heart disease, cancer and infectious diseases. **Plan, prepare and train** for safety at home and work. Your risk of death or injury from these everyday, mundane events is thousands of times greater than from any act of terrorism.

Brainstorm and think of other ideas. Use your **problem solving** abilities to come up with unique solutions. **Communicate** your ideas when and where appropriate.

The World Trade Center. Photo: Alan Friedman

The North Tower burns as a Boeing 767 strikes the South Tower.
Witnessed by millions of Americans (including the author) on live
TV. Photo: Associated Press

New York, NY, September 18, 2001 -- Falling steel I-beam spears an adjacent building like an arrow. Photo by Michael Rieger/ FEMA News Photo

New York, NY, September 15, 2001 -- The sun streams through the dust over the wreckage of the World Trade Center. Photo by Andrea Booher/FEMA News Photo

New York, NY, September 15, 2001 -- Firefighters take a break from working to clear rubble in downtown Manhattan following Tuesday's attack. Photo by Andrea Booher/FEMA News Photo

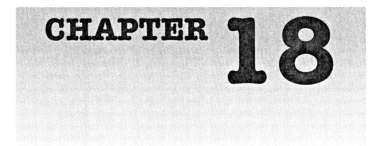

MAJOR CRISIS REVISTED:
St. Vincent's

S hortly after 8:45 am on September 11, St. Vincent's Hospital, a Level One Trauma Center in lower Manhattan, received a "code 3 alert". You could see the burning twin towers of The World Trade Center from the hospital's front door. Dr. Richard Westfall, Chief of Emergency Medicine at St. Vincent's, was paged and proceeded immediately to the emergency room. "A code 3 is a major disaster incident," said Dr. Westfall. "We were told an airplane hit the World Trade Center." All patients were instantly whisked upstairs to hospital beds. Within 20 minutes the ER was empty. A hush fell over the department as everyone waited, not quite knowing what to expect.

"I was here during the last (World Trade Center) bombing in 1993," remembered Westfall. "We were able to apply a lot of the lessons we learned from that." Patients began arriving around 9:30 am. The New York Fire Department had set up a command center on the scene and was triaging patients, sending the most critically injured first. Over the next 15 hours Dr. Westfall's **team** received 354 patients, including 55 major traumatic injuries, 2 traumatic cardiac arrests and 20 major burn victims (six of whom arrived simultaneously).

The ER hummed like a factory. A steady stream of ambulances flowed in, disgorging their damaged human cargo. Doctors and nurses swarmed over them, sorting the victims, resuscitating the injured, pronouncing the dead. The scene was one of frenetic but controlled chaos, filled with a multiplicity of activities that only made sense to the veterans of chaos who staff the ER. At midnight on September 11, a full 15 hours after it began, the parade of injured victims abruptly stopped. "Then," said Dr. Westfall, "We started to see the injured rescue workers. In a 72-hour period we saw a total of 510 patients."

Patient volume of this magnitude would easily overwhelm the normal capacity of even the busiest emergency room. But Westfall and the physicians, nurses and hospital administrators at St. Vincent's had learned their lessons well from the 1993 bombing, in which they had received over 200 patients. They had a well thought out **plan,** for which they had **prepared** and **trained** for 8 years. "Since '93 more attention was paid to the disaster **drills**. People took them seriously. They were conducted like a real disaster. In '93 we'd had a disaster drill 2 weeks before the bombing and it was a godsend."

The crux of the plan was to "decompress" the ER itself. In any emergency "room" the number of patients treated at one time is limited by the number of treatment areas, or "beds". St. Vincent's emergency staff rapidly expanded their treatment facility to include other parts of the hospital. They took charge of 12 beds in the surgical recovery room, 8 in the endoscopy suite, 8 dialysis beds and even set up 20 stretchers with portable oxygen in a gymnasium on the psychiatric ward. In addition to this, within an hour, 5 secondary treatment areas were set up. These were equipped with portable x-ray and were capable of caring for patients with less serious injuries. From the secondary areas patients were "discharged" to the hospital cafeteria, because there was no where else to go. Transportation in lower Manhattan was at a standstill. Patients kept coming in, but had no way to leave. As a result of the plan however, the staff was able to continually treat and move victims through. The ER itself did not succumb to patient gridlock, despite the daunting number of casualties.

Not only were there too many patients, but the crush of staff, many of whom were volunteers, was overwhelming as well. Dr. Westfall sent some of them out into the ambulance bay. "The weather was good, so we could do it. Doctors were shouting for and getting, specialty consultations right out in front of the ER (in the ambulance bay)."

Management of people was a key issue. The volunteer response from healthcare workers was phenomenal. Some 500 doctors and about as many nurses showed up and offered their services. Many were not even on staff at St Vincent's and had to have their credentials verified (a process that ordinarily takes weeks) before they could see patients. Two separate manpower "pools" were set up. One for doctors and one for nurses. Hospital administrators quickly confirmed credentials and the clinicians could then be sent wherever needed.

Medical records people came down to tag the patients and keep records. A radiologist was stationed in the ER to act as a consultant for immediate readings.

Logistics was facilitated by a "hot list" of suppliers who provided immediate shipments of bandages, supplies and equipment when the hospital ran low.

Communications was managed by 30 portable radios, which the hospital had purchased in 1993. St. Vincent's had been having a terrible problem with their telephone system that year and had rented the radios for auxiliary use until the phones were fixed. Fortuitously the radios were on hand during the 1993 bombing when the hospital switchboard was completely swamped by incoming calls. They worked so well that the hospital purchased the radios and made them part of the disaster plan. The radios continued to function when cell phone service and regular lines were jammed.

The **public** and the **media** were managed at a "family area" in a school one block from the hospital. This avoided interference with the treatment areas and helped take some of the load off the hospital's communications center.

Dr. Westfall also commented on the management of **emotions** once many of the patients with minor injuries were discharged. "We sent these people to the cafeteria because they had nowhere else to go. The patients had been traumatized (emotionally). They had this look in their eyes. We can deal with this (the emotional aspect) because of our training. We see this sort of thing every day - blood, severe burns, amputated limbs. These victims were in shock. At least in the cafeteria there was someone who could help them. There was one fire captain who came in. He'd had 21 men in his company. He lost them all. He came in looking for them. He was really distraught. I'll never forget the look in his eyes."

The medical crisis resulting from the September 11 attack on the World Trade Center was successfully **managed,** in part, due to lessons learned from the **crisis resolution** phase of the 1993 bombing. The disaster **plan** designed by St Vincent's Hospital was innovative and well thought out. It addressed vital issues that might not have otherwise been considered. To use Dr. Westfall's words, "Certain things you just don't know till you've been there." They were able to effectively **implement** the plan thanks to considerable **preparation and training**.

On Scene Triage

At the same time that St. Vincent's was clearing out it's emergency room, Dr. Joseph Ornato was sitting in a meeting room across the bridge in Brooklyn. " I was chairing an NIH (National Institutes of Health) meeting on public access to defibrillation. My practice is in Richmond Virginia, but I was formerly the paramedic coordinator at NYU Medical Center, so I'm pretty familiar with the city."

The building he was meeting in was evacuated, so Dr. Ornato and his group soon found themselves standing in the street, staring at the burning World Trade Center just across the river.

"Black smoke and flames were coming from both towers. People were pouring out of the subway tunnel, distraught. They had come from the World Trade Center. One woman was sobbing. She had just gotten into the subway beneath the Trade Center, dodging falling debris, as the tower collapsed. It was the last train out."

As the group stood watching, the wind changed and a dark cloud of debris headed towards them. They went into a hotel lobby to escape the cloud. Once inside the hotel the group reassembled and observed a moment of silence. Dr. Ornato looked around him. Nominally he was in charge of this group of about 150 people.

"Fifty of us were ER docs or paramedics. I've been running EMS (emergency medical services) for over 20 years. I knew we couldn't do any good at the hospitals because we were all from out of state and didn't have (New York) licenses."

So Ornato decided to see what he could do outside. He sent a few people to the Brooklyn Bridge to scout for casualties. Tens of thousands of people, many of them injured, were walking across the bridge into Brooklyn.

"Then I sent two big guys to the pharmacy. They just walked in, grabbed the pharmacist and told him they needed first aid supplies. Then they just took it, as much as they could carry."

Over the radio the group learned that the fire department had lost its command center (it was in the south tower). Shortly after that a fire lieutenant stopped to talk to the two doctors stationed at the Brooklyn Bridge. The fireman radioed his commander. Moments later he burst into the lobby of the hotel and flew up the escalator. He said, "We've commandeered a bus, are you willing to come over and help at the World Trade Center?"

"The next thing I know we've got a city bus and a police escort and 32 of my people are headed across the bridge to ground zero."

They arrived at the blast zone shortly thereafter and began setting up in a courtyard on Greenwich St. across from where the World Trade Center had been. The Marriott Hotel was on fire. There was dense smoke and dust.

"We set up in a semicircle of EMS (ambulance) units. At the start we had no equipment, nothing. They brought 40 conference room tables out of a financial building and we set them up as beds. I gave the firemen a list of what we needed and they brought it there. I asked for a MIRV (mobile intensive care) unit and they sent one over."

Dr. Ornato's **team** set up two critical care areas, a morgue and a work area for the chaplains and social workers. They stayed for over twelve hours, but after the initial wave of patients there was no one to be seen. Search and rescue efforts had been halted because of the instability of building 7 across the street.

"When building 7 collapsed the firemen yelled, 'Run!'—and we ran. It was a big cloud, like a wave, coming down the canyon between the buildings." Once the debris cloud cleared the triage team returned to the aid station from the shelter of the building lobby they had ducked into.

During their 12-hour vigil the triage team only treated 19 patients. "We were pretty angry and frustrated," said Ornato. "We were there, set up and ready. We would have been happy to be very busy, but there was nobody to treat."

Despite the tragic fact that most of the casualties never reached the triage station, this story emerges from the disaster as a heroic example of what can be done in an unexpected crisis with the proper **preparation** and **training**. It also illustrates the three principles of **assessment, decision, action.**

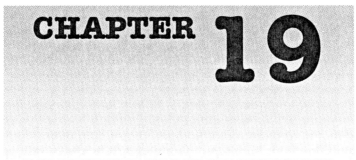

CHAPTER 19

BUSINESS CRISIS REVISTED

Morgan Stanley is an international financial brokerage firm with 700 offices throughout the United States and in 28 countries around the world. They employ over 63,000 people. The company has a market capitalization of more than $50 billion and manages in excess of $471 billion in assets for individuals, business, non-profit organizations and governments. Morgan Stanley was the largest tenant in the World Trade Center. Their offices filled the floors from 43 to 74 in the south tower, where 2700 of their people worked every day. Another 1000 people worked in number 5 World Trade Center, just adjacent to the towers. Although the World Trade Center office was not their headquarters, as some media reports have stated, it was a key operations center and was responsible for conducting much of the company's business.

Brett Galloway, Morgan Stanley's Vice President of Corporate Communications, told me that Morgan

Stanley developed a "contingency plan" at the time of the Gulf War in 1991. Because of bomb threats at that time, the question was posed, "What if the office was gone?" The thinking was that access to the office might be denied due to bomb threats. In response to this potential crisis the decision was made to develop a contingency back-up site. Suitable space was identified on Varick Street, not far from the twin towers and 400 computer workstations were installed. Aside from the workstations and basic furniture, the site was completely empty. Nobody worked there.

In 1993 when the first World Trade Center bomb incident occurred some of Morgan Stanley's people literally walked from the trade center offices over to Varick Street and went back to work. That attack occurred on a Friday. The following Monday Morgan Stanley's operation was up and running at the Varick Street location.

Even more basic to the Morgan Stanley "contingency plan" was their evacuation plan. This was revamped and redesigned in the aftermath of the 1993 bombing when, "Smoke was coming up the stairwells like a chimney." The crux of the plan was to get all their people out immediately. Floor wardens were designated on each floor. It was their responsibility to assure that everyone got out of the office immediately in the event of an emergency. No records or equipment were to be removed, people just needed to get out of the building. A video was made and circulated throughout the company to raise the awareness of all employees regarding the plans for reacting to emergencies. The plan and periodic updates was communicated and distributed to employees on a regular, ongoing basis.

All financial records were automatically backed

up on a regular basis and stored at several sites around the country and the world. This redundancy insured that Morgan Stanley and its clients would not lose vital records in the event of a catastrophe.

At 8:45 a.m. eastern standard time on September 11, 2001 workers heard an explosion and could see flames and smoke coming from the adjacent north tower. Shortly thereafter an official announcement from the New York Port Authority came over the public address system in the south tower. "This building is secure. Please return to your office." Officials, fearing that people would be hit by falling debris from the north tower, felt it would be safer for everyone to stay inside.

Despite the official announcement Morgan Stanley's decision had already been made. It was right in their plan. They would evacuate immediately. During the crucial next 18 minutes employees headed for the stairwells and started the long descent down the tower. Elevators were to be avoided because of the potential for becoming trapped due to a power failure or mechanical difficulties. At 9:03 a.m. eastern time, when the second Boeing 767 jet crashed into the south tower, right into the upper floors of Morgan Stanley's offices, floors 43 to 74 were essentially empty of workers. Morgan Stanley personnel were already far down the stairwells headed out of the building. When the plane hit people said they could feel the building sway from the impact. It took on average 30 to 60 minutes to complete the descent down the stairs. The stairwells became increasingly crowded as more and more people from the lower floors joined the exodus, yet there was little evidence of panic or hysteria during the evacuation.

Rick Rescorla, head of security for Morgan Stanley

was stationed in the stairwell with a megaphone. His calm demeanor helped to quell any sense of panic. He gave instructions, suggesting women take off their high-heeled shoes and generally projected a sense of controlled urgency. In the 1993 bombing incident he had been the final Morgan Stanley employee to leave the building. He was last seen in the stairwell giving instructions. Rick Rescorla is listed as missing and will be remembered as one of the heroes of September 11.

Louis Torres, another Morgan Stanley employee, was on his way down the stairwell when he heard a cry for help from one of the floors above. Louis turned around and climbed back up through the crowd to the 59th floor. There he found a woman on crutches who was unable to negotiate the stairs. Without hesitation, Louis hoisted the woman onto his back and carried her down 59 flights of stairs to safety.

In the immediate aftermath of the tragedy, Morgan Stanley faced the challenge of trying to account for all of the 3700 people working at the Trade Center. They **pulled out all the stops,** initiating an around the clock effort utilizing staff at their Discover Card call centers to field over 50,000 calls from people seeking or providing information. They **communicated** with their employees in New York and throughout the world via the company web-site (www.morganstanley.com) where specific information was posted for World Trade Center employees as well as general messages to the whole company and its customers.

By September 13, Morgan Stanley had accounted for all but 40 of their people. The final toll, of those missing and presumed dead, stands at 6. While even 6 deaths is a terrible tragedy, it could have been much worse. Phillip J. Purcell, Chairman and CEO of Morgan Stanley, in remarks broadcast to company employees on September 13, referred to the safe evacuation of nearly 3700 people as "miraculous." Although there was certainly some element of good fortune in the outcome, Morgan Stanley had been able to **tilt the odds** in their favor through careful **planning, preparation and training**.

From a business perspective the company didn't miss a beat. Operations were not interrupted. No records were lost. The next day people went to work at the Varick Street **"contingency"** site. An additional 500 computers were ordered immediately to accommodate employees. Another contingency backup site across the Hudson River in Jersey City, New Jersey was likewise activated. Employees were instructed to call their clients and reassure them that Morgan Stanley was sound and that no records or client funds had been affected.

Finally, in the **crisis resolution phase** of this disaster, Morgan Stanley has set up an employee assistance hot-line and arranged for group counseling for any of their employees who feel the need for it. The company has also established the "Morgan Stanley Victims Relief Fund (see the Resource section) for the benefit of Morgan Stanley employees, firefighters, police and other rescue workers.

TERRORISM AND TERROR:
The Psychology of Fear

Fear has been dealt with twice already in this book, in chapter 8 on Event Management and again in chapter 13 on Personal Skills. Why belabor the issue? Notwithstanding the fact that fear is a major challenge in the management of almost any crisis, I believe it is particularly important at this moment to address the use of fear as a weapon.

The objective of the terrorist is to achieve his goal by instilling fear. One dictionary definition of "terrorize" is "to coerce through intimidation." Violence and even more importantly, the threat of violence or other serious consequences, is used to cause the terrorist's victim to submit. The terrorist's hope is that his victim can be paralyzed by fear into complete inaction, putting the terrorist in complete control of the situation. Although we tend to think of terrorism as a political phenomenon it can be employed in the criminal, interpersonal or even business arena as well. When I was a kid we used to call terrorists "bullies". The game hasn't changed much since then, but the stakes are higher.

How do you deal with terrorism? To quote President Franklin Roosevelt, "We have nothing to fear but fear itself." Fear is actually what you need to fear and guard against, the most. Why is this so? Fear is your imagination run wild in a negative mode. Thinking of all the possible bad things that can happen may cause you to spend time energy and vital resources on unnecessary or even totally irrelevant matters. Worse yet you may be frightened into total inaction, essentially paralyzed by your fears. The terrorists' motto is, "Kill one person, frighten one million." If you can prevent yourself from succumbing to fear you have denied the terrorist his main objective.

Terrorism is often the tool of the outsider, the alienated, the disenfranchised minority. It is a means by which they can have maximum impact with a minimum expenditure of resources. Examples include the Red Brigades (West Germany), the Weathermen (US), the Irish Republican Army and the Shining Path (Peru). Alternatively, terror has been used by governments to control restive populations and suppress dissent. Witness the Stalinist period in the Soviet Union, the "Reign of Terror" during the French Revolution, Nazi Germany and present day Iraq. Terror is routinely employed by criminals to cow their victims into submissive cooperation.

What can you do to defuse this time bomb of fear and render the terrorist's most important weapon impotent? The first step is to recognize fear as a weapon and understand its objective. The next step is to learn how to deal with it.

Fortunately, a biological model of terror is readily available. There is a well-known syndrome, which is seen quite frequently by emergency physicians, known as "panic disorder". The hapless victim of this syndrome experiences a constellation of symptoms basically identical to full-blown terror without any rational precipitating cause. It may occur when he is driving a car, at home, at work, or even lying in bed. His heart begins to race. Breathing quickens. The patient may begin to sweat. He may experience chest pain, dizziness, feel faint or lightheaded. The patient may actually fall to the ground unconscious. Mentally he is experiencing the sensation of intense fear, terror, even impending death. The first time these patients present to the doctor they think they are having a heart attack or some other medical catastrophe. Often they get admitted to the hospital or even the cardiac surveillance unit. On subsequent visits the patients may begin to question the competence of the physician, who can find no "real reason" for the symptoms. They may begin to question their own sanity. Eventually they may limit their activities out of fear of having an attack.

For some unknown reason these patients are experiencing a sudden, "fight or flight", adrenaline response. The problem is that there is no threat present to respond to. After doing a battery of tests to rule out any underlying disease process I sit down and talk to these patients at length. I explain first of all that they are actually not in any danger when this "attack" occurs. I immediately add that this is a very real physiologic phenomenon, which can be reproduced in most patients by the infusion of certain psychoactive chemicals. It is not "all in their head" and they are not "crazy". Next the patient must learn how to deal with the attacks when they occur.

Sometimes medication is necessary. Often the knowledge of what is happening is enough to allow the patient to control his fear, calm himself and abort the attack.

At times everyone experiences some lesser sort of panic reaction. It may occur when you get up in front of a large group to speak or perform. This is known as stage fright. It may happen in response to a challenging situation at home or at work, such as an argument. It also may occur, quite appropriately, in the setting of a very real physical threat.

The point of all this is that you can learn to control fear and panic from real threats the same way patients with panic disorder control unreal ones. Use the techniques outlined in previous chapters for the management of emotions. Calm yourself so that you can think rationally in order to **assess, decide and act**. Your ability to think under pressure will deny the terrorist an easy victory.

Once you have dealt with the issue of your own emotions you must logically move on to deal with the fears of others and of society as a whole. Panic is contagious. So is calm. Confident, steady leadership can work wonders in a crisis. You have seen many examples already in this book. Many more are available throughout history and contemporary events. Think of the solid, seemingly fearless, performances of Winston Churchill during the Second World War, or of Abraham Lincoln during the Civil War. Despite very real personal fears and reservations, these men stood up and spoke words of confidence and hope that inspired millions.

Fear has been used as an effective weapon of war before. During the War of 1812, the British Frigate La Hogue anchored off the seacoast town of Scituate,

Massachusetts, 30 miles south of Boston. Seemingly a sleepy fishing village, Scituate's North River was a major colonial center of shipbuilding. The warship launched two barges filled with redcoats with orders to capture, sack and burn the town.

Abigail and Rebecca Bates, two young daughters of the Scituate lighthouse keeper observed the British landing party. Picking up a fife and drum, they hid behind a thick clump of cedar trees and loudly played military music. The redcoats, fearing the landing would be opposed by a regiment of militia, returned to their ship and sailed back to Boston. This victory by the "army of two" became a local legend.

In the waning days of the Second World War the Japanese military put up ferocious resistance as American forces approached their home islands. Kamikaze, suicide air attacks and a military code of fighting to the death was calculated to instill the fear of huge casualties during any attack on the home islands of Japan itself. The Japanese hoped this would result in a negotiated peace and avert total surrender. This fear of casualties played a role in President Truman's decision to drop two atomic bombs on Japan. That in turn resulted in the Japanese surrender due to fear of total annihilation in a nuclear holocaust. They didn't know that at the time the United States only had two such bombs. Propaganda and actions designed to inspire fear have been utilized as weapons in just about every war before and since.

Be wary of the **media**. As we have stated previously, the media is one of those factors that needs to be **managed.** The media looks for drama. They want to show the controversial or sensational situation. The graphic media (especially television) wants a good visual event. They like to show things exploding, disintegrating, blowing away in the wind. There's nothing worse, in their view, than a hurricane that fails to provide severe, highly visible damage, or a fire that gets extinguished before the camera crew arrives. The media is like this not because they are awful, sadistic voyeurs. The media simply reflects what they think the audience wants to see. Even in the process of writing this book I have looked hard for dramatic examples to illustrate my points. If I utilized boring and routine situations would you have read the book, or even picked it up? It would have contained the same lessons, but been much less interesting to read.

You must be careful not to allow the media to distort your understanding of events. Whenever possible get information from primary sources, or objective, unbiased observers. This can be very difficult, especially in instances where an event occurs far away, or in an area where you have limited expertise. Try to compare information from different sources to discern its validity. Remember all observers are biased in one way or another.

An interesting exercise is to read an article or view a report concerning an area in which you posses particular expertise. How accurate is the reporting based on what you know? What makes you think it is any more accurate in areas in which you are not an expert? For example, for several days during the anthrax scare of October 2001 everyone on the television news was referring to anthrax as a "virus". In fact, it is a bacterium (Bacillus anthracis). The distinction may be lost on the non-scientists among you, but it has important implications for prevention, treatment, spread of the disease and viability of the organisms. One person in the media made a mistake and everyone else followed right along and repeated it, simply reporting the same "news" over and over again. By the tenth time you hear it you figure it has to be the truth.

You must also be cautious that the media does not precipitate crisis fatigue, or even depression. The constant parade of terrible images of death, disease and destruction can have a detrimental effect on even the most positive observer. It is very easy to feel that doom is approaching and that your side is losing if all you see and hear is "bad news".

Why am I spending so much energy "bashing" the media in a chapter on terrorism? Because the media is an important tool of the terrorist. How can they frighten you if you cannot see or hear what they have done? Do you think it was accidental that the second airplane flew into the south tower of the World Trade Center on live TV? Why was anthrax specifically sent to newspaper and TV reporters? What better way to get instant and widespread attention? To paraphrase Franklin Roosevelt, "We have nothing to fear but fear itself and television."

Do I advocate censorship or ignorance of current events? Absolutely not. I do think that you must understand that the media chooses what is sensational or "newsworthy" in their eyes. Whether the reporting is balanced or not depends on their sources, preconceived notions, prejudices and the quality of images available. It is up to politicians and other "newsmakers" to do their best to be candid and constructive in providing "stories". It is up to the media to be responsible in selecting and reporting them. It is up to you to be skeptical and critical. Above all, use your **judgment** in reading, listening to, or viewing the "news".

What can the average person do about terrorism? Don't give in to it. Refuse to alter your life. Continue to travel. Go about your normal activities as you have in the past. Despite the images and stories you see in the media you are at much greater risk each time you get in your car, than you are flying in an airplane. Practice **crisis prevention**. Buckle your seat belt every time you drive. You are at a thousand times greater risk of death from pneumococcal pneumonia than you are from anthrax. There's a vaccine for pneumococcal pneumonia. Have you been vaccinated?*

The point is you need to use your **judgment**. Analyze and weigh the true **risk**. Refuse to give in to **fear**.

---

*(footnote: This is somewhat controversial. Officially, right now most physicians are vaccinating children, adults with chronic disease and people over 65. In my opinion every adult should be vaccinated.)

DISASTER

What's the difference between a crisis and a disaster? Earlier we defined crisis as a sudden turning point or critical change. Disaster on the other hand is defined as, "An event causing great distress or ruin; sudden and crushing misfortune." A disaster can certainly be regarded as a crisis. Alternatively in chapter 9, on Major Crisis, we referred to the Amtrak rail crash as a "disaster." Is every crisis a disaster? That may depend on your point of view. Is it happening to you or to someone else? In some sense this may be an artificial distinction, but for didactic purposes we will reserve the word "disaster" for catastrophic events of large magnitude. These typically involve many thousands or even millions of people and affect whole societies, or large geopolitical units·such as countries. The principles of crisis management apply to large-scale disasters no less than such laws of nature as gravity. The challenge is to recognize and apply them on such a grand scale.

Dr. Donald Walsh was visiting Turkey as part of an emergency medical services training group in the summer of 1999. As if on cue, the group was provided with an all too real example for their teaching purposes. At 3:00 a.m. local time on August 17, the earth moved. This earthquake, which registered 7.4 on the Richter scale and lasted for an incredible 48 seconds, has been called the worst of the twentieth century. The magnitude of the quake coupled with its unusually long duration and the fact that it struck in heavily populated areas combined to cause great destruction and loss of life.

The Richter scale is a seismographic measurement of the energy released in an earthquake that is based on a logarithmic scale of the seismic wave amplitude. Translating the Richter scale number into the amount of energy released we find that an increase of 1 whole unit on the scale (say from 6 to 7) reflects a tenfold (one power of ten) increase in wave amplitude. This in turn translates mathematically (when you convert wave amplitude into the actual measurement of energy) into a 31-fold increase in energy released*.

The Northridge Earthquake in California in 1994, which caused 57 deaths and $30 billion in damage, was a magnitude 6.7 earthquake. This quake was a 7.4, releasing almost 22 times as much energy.

The earthquake's epicenter was on the Anatolian Fault, at Izmit in northwestern Turkey. Shock waves traveled out from there at an amazing 33,000 miles per hour and shook buildings in Ankara, the capitol and Istanbul on Turkey's western shore. The shock waves, propagating through the earth in sinusoidal

*(footnote: according to information from the US Geographic Survey posted on their web-site @USGS.gov).

fashion, toppled alternating rows of buildings in an eerie hopscotch pattern as if those left standing had been spared by some unseen hand.

In 48 seconds 16,000 people died, 200,000 were injured and 600,000 were left homeless. In one area along the Sea of Marmara a 300-foot wide swath of the coastline, including many hotels and vacation homes, sank into the sea. Tourists were drowned in their hotel room beds. Everyone was asleep when the earthquake struck. People were trapped naked, or in their bedclothes, by the fallen ceilings and walls of their rooms. Thousands were crushed to death in their sleep.

This country of 64 million people was totally devastated by the quake. Turkey, a NATO member with one foot in Europe and the other in Asia is a land of many contradictions. It is a country were "everyone has a cell phone but there is no running water." Many of the buildings that collapsed were built with a 2:1 sand to concrete mixture instead of the standard 1:1 mix. They had not been built according to the building code because, "There was no code." A number of building contractors left the country in the aftermath of the quake.

The firemen in each locality, who were responsible for search and rescue, were decimated along with the rest of the population. Their trucks and equipment lay crushed under the rubble of collapsed firehouses. The local infrastructure was in shambles. Petroleum fires burned in the industrial areas. Roads and power lines had been disrupted. Twenty-five hundred buildings had fallen down. Another 9,000 were in such bad shape they had to be demolished. The entire population of the region was in need of shelter, water, food, clothing and basic sanitation. There was a serious risk of infectious disease and winter, which can be harsh in this part of the world, was not far away.

Dr. Walsh, who had been there to teach, was pressed into service. He traveled from town to town throughout the region giving advice, counsel and support to local fire-chiefs and rescue workers. His description is both stark and chilling. "I was driven along the coast for 200 miles and saw nothing but mass destruction. Whole towns had been wiped out. I asked myself, when is this devastation going to stop?"

Firemen were pulling people from the rubble, handing off the live ones to the Red Crescent and then going right back to digging. They were too busy digging to transport the injured to the hospital. Family members and neighbors often formed the only rescue crews when firemen were unavailable. Rescuers crawled into "caves" formed by collapsed buildings to extricate those still alive. Hands and feet could frequently be seen protruding from collapsed buildings. The dead began decaying beneath the rubble where they lay.

This is not a story with a happy ending. Turkey was totally unprepared for a disaster of this magnitude. There was no plan and little in the way of resources to deal with the aftermath of the earthquake. Thousands suffered through the harsh winter in tent cities with little heat or protection from the elements. To this day the recovery process still goes on. On a positive note, Dr. Walsh, on retainer to the government of Turkey, drew up a national disaster plan. In the future there will at least be a plan. Turkey also received significant aid from its neighbors including Greece, Russia and Israel. This humanitarian response may have helped political relations in the region.

The lessons of this story bear careful review. Do your governmental, organizational and personal crisis plans have provisions for a disaster of this magnitude? Are you prepared logistically for such a catastrophic event? Do you have the requisite personal survival skills and training?

You don't think a catastrophe of this magnitude can occur where you live? Think again. Earthquake records in the United States date back only about 250 years, yet during that time period a damaging earthquake has occurred in virtually every state east of the Mississippi. In 1755 an earthquake of Richter scale 6 off Cape Ann heavily damaged Boston. During the winter of 1811 – 1812 three earthquakes of 8.4 to 8.7 on the Richter scale occurred in New Madrid, Missouri. Shock waves from this quake were so strong that observers reported seeing the land distorted in visible, rolling waves. They changed the course of the Mississippi River and rang church bells in Boston and Washington DC. In 1866 a quake of magnitude 6.6 virtually leveled Charleston, South Carolina.

An earthquake in the heavily populated areas of the eastern United States would be especially devastating. Building codes there are not as strict as they are in California and there are more old, pre-code buildings.

Aside from earthquakes there are also violent storms, fires, floods and other forms of disaster. I say all this not to frighten you, but to make you aware. **A crisis will occur**.

CRISIS RESOLUTION

The resolution phase of the Marmara earthquake crisis is still going on. The rebuilding of infrastructure and housing will take many years. The rebuilding of people's lives and society may take years as well. In the tent city refugee camps set up in the aftermath of the quake, Dr. Walsh describes "a look in people's eyes" symptomatic of despair. These were people, possessing little to begin with, who had lost everything. They had no homes; just the clothing on their backs and those things given to them by relief agencies. Only in the eyes of children did he see the light of hope.

As part of crisis resolution, Walsh attempted to introduce the concept of debriefing, to help people ventilate, air their feelings and deal with their grief. "We've found CID (critical incident debriefing) to play a very important role in EMS", said Walsh. It allows people to get feelings out in the open which otherwise remain bottled up inside contributing to burnout and, potentially, to future impairment.

His effort was met by cold rejection from the firemen. Questionnaires were sent out to the firemen and they refused to fill them out. "They all felt that the earthquake was God's will and that they were being punished." They did not wish to talk about the events of the disaster, or even think about it. Nurses at the hospitals, on the other hand, essentially demanded debriefing. They wanted to air their feelings and deal with them.

"One 9 year-old girl, the daughter of a fire chief, had lost her best friend in the earthquake. She wrote letters to her dead friend for weeks. This was her way of dealing with the pain. She basically debriefed herself."

In another cautionary note from the crisis resolution phase, Dr. Walsh personally developed pneumoconiosis, a persistent pneumonia-like illness, from dust inhalation following the earthquake. He has since recovered.

August 17, 1999 at 3 am along the Marmara Coast of Turkey, the earth moved. Sinusoidal shock-waves toppled alternating rows of buildings. All photos this chapter: Dr. Donald Walsh

People were trapped naked or in their bedclothes by the fallen walls and ceilings of their rooms.

Rescue trucks and equipment lay crushed under the rubble of
collapsed firehouses.

Petroleum fires burned in industrial areas.
Local infrastructure was in shambles.

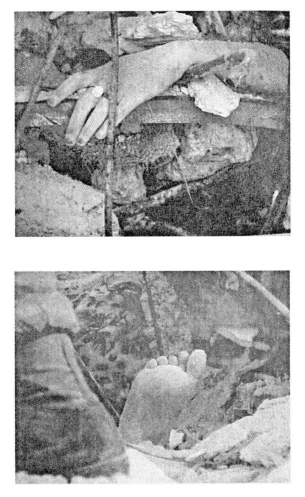

Hands and feet could be seen protruding from collapsed buildings.

ADDITIONAL TECHNIQUES

In this Chapter we will touch upon a variety of specific situations and techniques which may be useful in certain instances.

CRISIS TIMING

The first of these is the concept of **timing** a crisis. This is useful in a situation where a particular crisis is inevitable. It's just a question of when, not if, it will occur. In this case it may be useful to actually precipitate the crisis, in order to cause it to occur at the most favorable time.

A real life example of this is avalanche management. At ski resorts in areas where the mountains are particularly steep and the snow very deep avalanches are a common danger. You only need to see the aftermath, an entire mountainside of trees, boulders and snow deposited over a road or a village, to understand the awesome power of this act of nature. An avalanche occurring while people are skiing can be a deadly disaster.

The ski resort people know that this will occur and often exactly where and when based on experience. Therefore they detonate explosive charges in the snow, causing the avalanche to occur early in the morning before skiers go to the slopes. By causing frequent, small avalanches preventively, at a time when no one is in danger, they are reducing the risk of large unplanned avalanches on a mountainside covered with skiers later in the day.

CRISIS AVOIDANCE

Sometimes you may be given the choice of **walking away** from a crisis. This choice should be weighed carefully. You may have some responsibility to be involved in this crisis. To walk away might be unethical, immoral, or even illegal. Such words as negligence, desertion and abandonment come to mind. Alternatively this crisis might represent a great opportunity to prove yourself to your business partners, family, friends, or the community. It might be an opportunity to help your fellow man or to help yourself gain some real reward or advantage.

On the other hand this crisis may be a dangerous, unmitigated disaster, with little or nothing to gain in it and no real responsibility on your part.

How can you tell the difference? Often you can tell by exercising good **judgment**. This may not be easy, so consider carefully.

One example might be a job offer at a company that is failing rapidly. I know of a case in which someone spent a year as a hospital administrator intern after finishing the prescribed course of study. At the end of the year the hospital liked this person so much she was offered the job of president of the hospital, which she immediately accepted.

The following year the hospital went into receivership and closed. In retrospect and probably even prospectively, the closing was inevitable. I doubt this looked good on the administrator's resume. Would she have been faulted for just walking away and declining the job? I don't think so. Did she see it as a huge opportunity that would jump start her career? Perhaps, but if she did she was mistaken. Was accepting the job an example of poor **judgment**? Probably it was. She could have just walked away.

Ask the question. Is this really your crisis? Do you want to make it your crisis? You may have the option to decline the challenge. Do your research carefully. Make a thorough **assessment** before you **decide**.

CONFLICT MANAGEMENT

The management of conflict was not covered in the chapter on event management. Nevertheless, we know from crisis recognition that conflict is commonly present in a crisis. Conflicts may exist between you and the opposition, between members of your own team, between you and the media, or with other interested parties to the crisis situation. Basic principles relating to conflict include the following:

1. Whenever possible avoid a fight if you are not likely to win, or if the cost of winning is prohibitive.
2. Learn to utilize negotiation as an effective means of dealing with conflict.

3. Never embarrass the other party in public.
4. If conflict becomes inevitable use overwhelming force to defeat the opposition before they have a chance to harm you (or themselves).
5. Don't make enemies unnecessarily.

The emergency room is an almost constant cauldron of conflict. There are conflicts between the doctor and the patients, between doctors, between nurses and doctors, nurses and nurses, patients and their families, families and the nurses, between virtually any of the "players" present in the ER. How do we deal with it? Review rules 1 through 5 above.

A simple example of rule #1 is the patient who wants a cigarette. You and I both know that smoking cigarettes is bad for you. The patient knows it too. My first tack therefore is to tell the patient that cigarettes are bad for you and that smoking is prohibited in the ER. This usually works. However in the case of a serious nicotine addict, someone who is mentally ill, or both, it may not. What might happen? The patient might become agitated and elect to leave and not get treatment for his problem or at a minimum disrupt the delivery of care. If it's not absolutely dangerous (someone having chest pain or on oxygen) I often let them go outside and smoke (with an escort when indicated).

A more ancient and negative example of rule #1 was provided by Phyrrhus, the king of Epirus. In 280 BC Phyrrus sailed to Italy with 25,000 men and 20 elephants. He engaged the Romans at Heraclea and won a victory which cost him most of his army. Eventually Phyrrhus returned to Epirus with about a third of his original troops. This did not make

Phyrrhus very popular amongst his people. Hence was coined the term, "Phyrrhic victory".

Rule #2, the ability to use negotiation to defuse or allay conflict is of critical importance. Negotiation is listed as an important personal skill in chapter 13. It is also an important organizational skill and one of the skills of a good leader. I suggest you obtain one or several books on the topic and do some reading.

My favorite story about negotiation and conflict management involved a fight over an egg. One morning my two young sons were arguing loudly over who was going to eat the only remaining egg in the refrigerator for breakfast. Stepping in with the fatherly wisdom of Solomon I sagely suggested they cook the egg and divide it in equal halves. This satisfied neither of them and the argument continued as loudly as before. They each demanded the whole egg. I was becoming annoyed. They had both rejected a perfectly reasonable negotiated settlement. I checked my immediate impulse, which was to get angry and join the argument myself and shifted into "negotiation mode". Cautiously I inquired as to their "real needs". To my astonishment I discovered that one of them wanted the whole yolk while the other wanted only the white of the egg. The egg was immediately hard-boiled and the matter settled to the total satisfaction of both parties.

Rule #3 involves a matter of common courtesy and common sense. It also relates directly to rule #5. People will forgive all sorts of things done in private, but public humiliation may gain you an enemy for life. Not only that, by diminishing another person's status in public you immediately diminish your own. Other people will remember your behavior long after they have forgiven the person you have publicly embarrassed. I make it a point to take students aside when correcting them, out of earshot of patients and staff. It can be detrimental to the morale of staff and the confidence of patients in their caregivers to do otherwise.

Rule #4 often comes into play with patients who are psychotic, intoxicated, jacked up on stimulants, or just plain angry. Most assaultive patients can be easily overcome by six or eight nurses armed with leather restraints and the appropriate injectable sedative solution. We surround and swarm them the same way Gulliver was overcome by the Liliputians.

Even the most dangerous and physically imposing of patients generally becomes docile in the face of several large armed policemen, summoned at my behest by the ward clerk. I have never seen the police forced to resort to violence in such a confrontation. To quote one such suddenly subdued patient, "I may be crazy, but I ain't stupid."

On the geopolitical stage a good example of rule #4 was in evidence during the Gulf War. President Bush skillfully and patiently assembled an overwhelming military force before beginning an attack that rapidly subdued the defending Iraqis. This was also a good example of crisis timing.

Rule #5 relates in part to rule #3. People under stress, as they often are in the emergency room, will say and do things they later regret. It pays always to be courteous, calm and polite. Try to keep conflict on a professional or business level. Avoid making it into a "personal" issue.

Oftentimes patients in the emergency room elect not to follow my advice. Yet, more than one patient has sincerely thanked me for my help and concern, even as they signed out of the ER against medical advice. Even your opponents will respect you if you can remain objective and unbiased in the heat of the moment. Channel your anger into positive action as discussed under the management of emotions. In many real life situations, as in politics, your current opponent may be needed in the future as an ally. Avoid making too many enemies. You don't need more people out there looking for ways to harm you or your career.

SUMMARY

If you have finished reading this book you have made a good start. In order to obtain the full benefit of it **you must go back and do the exercises**. Make the 3X5 cards and lists.

Now, take a moment and review what you've learned:

A crisis will occur.

You are always either in **crisis or pre-crisis**.

Crisis is recognizable by its signs and symptoms: **Change, conflict, decision, consequences, uncertainty, fear.**

Crisis is sometimes **predictable** and sometimes **preventable**. You must work to understand **risk factors, decrease risk and uncertainty** and **mitigate injury**.

You must develop and use good **judgment**.

You must **plan, prepare and train**.

You must learn to **solve problems** and deal with **mistakes**.

You must teach yourself to **manage** by adopting the mode of **assessment, decision, action**.

You must master **personal and organizational skills**.

Learn from your own crisis through **crisis resolution**.

Learn from post mortems about the **fatal mistakes** of others.

Practice, practice, practice.

Remember: A crisis will occur.

AFTERWORD

It is not my intent in writing this book to depress or demoralize people by recounting all the sad, evil or tragic events occurring in the world. On the contrary, my aim is to motivate the reader to gain confidence through knowledge and the acquisition of skills. I have tried to balance the negative stories with positive ones, as well as point out the positive aspects of negative events whenever possible. The plain truth however, is that not all stories turn out well in the real world.

I hope I have conveyed the message that courage and a positive attitude in the face of adversity will oftentimes make a difference. If the alternative is giving up, why not try?

Constructive criticism and feedback from readers is welcomed and should be directed to my email address: markedoc02@aol.com.

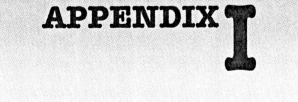

JOHNSON AND JOHNSON CREDO

We believe our first responsibility is to the doctors, nurses and patients, to mothers and all others who use our products and services. In meeting their needs everything we do must be of high quality. We must consistently strive to reduce our costs in order to maintain reasonable prices. Customers' orders must be serviced promptly and accurately. Our suppliers and distributors must have an opportunity to make a fair profit.

We are responsible to our employees, the men and women who work with us throughout the world. Everyone must be considered as an individual. We must respect their dignity and recognize their merit. They must have a sense of security in their jobs. Compensation must be fair and adequate and working conditions clean orderly and safe. Employees must feel free to make suggestions and complaints. There must be equal opportunity for employment, development and advancement for those qualified.

We must provide competent management and their actions must be just and ethical.

We are responsible to the communities in which we live and work and to the world community as well. We must be good citizens – support good works and charities and bear our fair share of taxes. We must encourage civic improvements and better health and education. We must maintain in good order the property we are privileged to use, protecting the environment and natural resources.

Our final responsibility is to our stockholders. Business must make a sound profit. We must experiment with new ideas. Research must be carried on, innovative programs developed and mistakes paid for. New equipment must be purchased, new facilities provided and new products launched. Reserves must be created to provide for adverse times. When we operate according to these principles, the stockholders should realize a fair return.

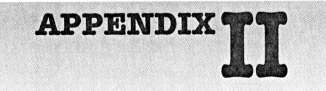

APPENDIX II

FAMILY DISATER PREPAREDNESS PLAN

(Adapted from information supplied by FEMA)

List potential disaster situations.
Create a family crisis plan.
Complete the emergency checklist.
Practice and maintain your plan.

What potential disasters are likely to happen to you? Some, such as fire, can happen virtually anywhere. Others, like hurricanes, floods, tornadoes, or tidal waves, are more common in certain geographic regions. Contact your local Red Cross or emergency management office. Obtain a list of historically common disasters in your area. Get specific information on how to prepare for each of them. Learn about your community's emergency warning signals. What do they sound like? What should you do when you hear them? Inquire regarding disaster plans where you work, at your children's school and other facilities where your family spends time. Look into special issues that may affect you, such as provisions for the elderly, the disabled, or pets.

Create a disaster plan. Meet with your family and discuss why you need to prepare. Some convincing may be necessary to get them to take this seriously. Perhaps they should read this book. Devise specific and generic plans. These should include meeting places and methods of communication in the event your house is gone or inaccessible. Discuss various disaster scenarios and the concept of teamwork. Establish an out of state friend or family member as a "contact person" in the event of a regional disaster. Discuss what to do in case of an evacuation.

Complete this emergency checklist.

- Post emergency numbers (fire, police, ambulance, contacts) by the phone.
- Teach small children how to dial 911 or the appropriate local emergency number.
- Show everyone how to turn off the gas, water and electricity.
- Check to make sure your insurance coverage is adequate.
- Keep fire extinguishers handy and get training in how to use them.
- Install smoke detectors on every level, especially near bedrooms.
- Conduct a home hazard survey.
- Stock emergency / disaster supplies.
- Take a first aid / CPR course.
- Determine home escape routes, two from each room.
- Identify safe places within the home for appropriate shelter in disasters.
- Practice and maintain your plan. Quiz your family periodically (every 6 months).

- Conduct fire and evacuation drills. Replace stored water and food periodically.
- Test and recharge fire extinguishers according to the manufacturers specifications.
- Test smoke detectors regularly and replace batteries at least annually.

EARTHQUAKE/DISASTER PREPAREDNESS CHECKLIST
(adapted from information from the U.S. Geographic Survey, Dept. of the Interior)

PLANNING
- Be familiar with the earthquake risk for your region.
- Draw up a simple family disaster plan, including a family meeting place and communication plan.
- Learn about regional and local earthquake / disaster plans.
- Discuss mutual aid in a disaster with your neighbors.

PREPARATION
- Know the location of local police and fire station.
- Know the locations of utility connections (gas, electricity, water) and how to turn them off.
- Assemble a Disaster Kit with the following:

_____ Fire extinguisher – familiarize yourself and family with its use.
_____ First aid kit
_____ Flashlights with extra batteries and bulbs
_____ Portable radio with extra batteries
_____ Three day supply of drinking water (minimum 1gal/person/day)
_____ Water purification tablets and/or bleach (and instructions in appropriate dilution)
_____ Canned and dried food for several days (mechanical can opener).
_____ Camp stove or barbecue grill (and charcoal)
_____ Waterproof heavy-duty plastic bags.
_____ Tent, tarpaulin or other portable shelter
_____ Blankets or sleeping bags

- Keep these supplies together in a safe, accessible location.

TRAINING
- Learn (both you and your family) first aid.
- Learn basic survival skills.

EVENT MANAGEMENT (In a real earthquake)
- Indoors—Get under a sturdy table or other piece of furniture and hang on to it. Stay clear of windows, brick chimneys, heavy furniture or appliances (or anything that might fall on you). Don't run downstairs or rush outside.

You might fall or be hit by a falling object.

- Outdoors—Stay in the open. Get away from trees, utility poles, buildings, power lines, or anything else that might fall on you.
- In your car—Stop carefully as far out of traffic as possible. Do not stop on a bridge, under an overpass or near anything that may fall on the car. Stay inside the car.
- Afterwards—Expect aftershocks. Watch out for hazards: open gas lines, fires, electric wires, weakened structures. Don't turn the gas back on. Assemble your supplies. Keep the freezer and refrigerator shut as much as possible to preserve food if the power is out. Avoid drinking unsafe water or eating spoiled or contaminated food. Maintain basic sanitation. Help your neighbors.

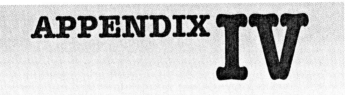

HOME FIRST AID KIT

(Adapted from material available from ACEP)

_____ First Aid Manual

Medicines:
_____ Acetaminophen, Ibuprofen, Aspirin
_____ Cough medicine (with
       dextromethorphan)
_____ Antihistamine (Benadryl or similar
       medication)
_____ Decongestant (Sudafed)
_____ Hydrocortisone cream
_____ Calamine lotion
_____ Activated charcoal and Syrup of
       Ipecac (on advice of physician)
_____ Oral rehydration fluids (for pediatric
       age groups)
_____ Oral medicine syringe (for babies)

Wound care supplies:

_____ Bandages and Band-Aids in various sizes

_____ Wound closure tapes (butterflies)

_____ Triangular bandages (slings)

_____ Elastic (ace) wrap

_____ Sterile gauze rolls and pads (2X2 &4X4)

_____ Adhesive tape

_____ Scissors

_____ Safety pins

_____ Antiseptic solution and wipes

_____ Cold packs (chemical activated or ice pack)

_____ Safety pins

_____ Tweezers (forceps)

_____ Rubber gloves

Additional Items:

_____ Anti-bacterial soap

_____ Lubricating jelly

_____ Digital (non-mercury containing) thermometer

_____ Splints (for fractures)

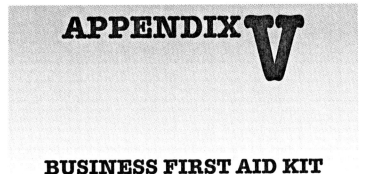

APPENDIX V

BUSINESS FIRST AID KIT

Everything in the home first aid kit in proportion to the number of employees.

_____ An AED (automatic external defibrillator) and training in its use.

_____ Aspirin (the first drug given in a heart attack)

_____ Stretcher

_____ Back (spine) board

_____ Rigid cervical collar

_____ Specialized equipment based on specific business related hazards.

DISASTER/WILDERNESS
FIRST AID KIT

Everything in the home first aid kit plus:
_____ Duct tape (for use with improvised splints)
_____ Motion sickness medicine

SURVIVAL KIT

BASIC KIT

_____ Water (bottled)
_____ Water purification tablets or filter
_____ Canteen or plastic containers for water
_____ Dried or preserved food
_____ Matches in a waterproof container
_____ Candles
_____ First aid kit
_____ Pocketknife
_____ Rope / string
_____ Duct tape
_____ Flashlight
_____ Compass
_____ Signal mirror
_____ Whistle
_____ Rain-gear
_____ Hat

ADVANCED KIT
The basic kit plus:

_____ More water
_____ More food
_____ Flare gun and flares
_____ Survival manual
_____ Wire (for snares)
_____ Fishing equipment
_____ All in one tool (pliers, knife ,
        screwdriver, awl , etc.) such as a
        "Leatherman" tool
_____ Shovel, ax, saw
_____ Fishing equipment
_____ Insect netting / repellent
_____ Sunscreen
_____ Tarp or tent
_____ Camp stove and fuel
_____ Lantern
_____ Fry pan and large pot
_____ More duct tape
_____ More rope

COLD WEATHER KIT
All of the above plus:

_____ Warm sleeping bag
_____ Warm clothing
_____ More matches

WATER / MARINE KIT

_____ Raft, repair kit, paddles
_____ Personal flotation device (life jacket)
_____ Hat
_____ Bailer
_____ Fluorescent dye marker
_____ Desalination kit (ocean)

APPENDIX  VIII

DEALING WITH MEDICAL EMERGENCIES

PREVENTION
- Do what you can to stay healthy by routine health maintenance.
- Eliminate hazards from your home.
- Avoid risky behaviors.

PLANNING, PREPARATION AND TRAINING
- Have a home emergency medical plan.
- Post emergency numbers by the phone including 911 or its local alternative, the number for the poison control center, your personal physician and family contact numbers.
- Take a first aid course including CPR.
- Purchase or assemble a home first aid kit (see Appendix IV).

RECOGNITION

- Learn the signs and symptoms of common medical emergencies (ideally during a first aid course). Learn signs and symptoms which may pertain to illnesses or conditions specific to you or your family.
- Common medical emergencies include: severe bleeding, difficulty breathing, chest pain, sudden weakness or dizziness, severe headache, severe pain, persistent vomiting and diarrhea, altered mental status, suicidal behavior.

ASSESSMENT, DECISION, ACTION

- If by your assessment this is a real medical emergency get help immediately.
- Call 911 or summon assistance by shouting or any means necessary.
- Give first aid while awaiting assistance and during transportation to the emergency room.

INDEX

REFERENCES AND RESOURCES

Advanced Cardiac Life Support. American Heart Association, National Center. 7272 Greenville Avenue, Dallas, TX 75231-4596. 2000.

Aircraft Accident Report. United Airlines Flight 232, Sioux City, Iowa. July 19, 1989 National Transportation Safety Board.

American College of Emergency Physicians (ACEP) First Aid Handbook. Jon R. Krohmer, American College of Emergency Physicians.

Carnegie, Dale. How to Win Friends and Influence People. Pocket Books, Simon and Schuster. 1230 Avenue of the Americas, New York, NY 10020. 1964.

Cohen, Herbert. You Can Negotiate Anything. Lyle Stuart Inc. Secaucus, NJ. 1980.

Emergency Management Guide for Business and Industry. Federal Emergency Management Agency. October 1993.

Fisher, Michael. Guide to Clinical Preventive Services. William and Wilkins. 428 East Preston St. Baltimore, MD 21202. 1989.

Fisher, Roger and Ury, William. Getting to Yes (Negotiating Agreement) Penguin Books.40 W 23rd St. New York, NY 10010. 1983.

Graham, Benjamin. Preventing Automobile Injury. Auburn House Publishing Company. Dover, MA 1988.

Hall, Jack and Zwemer, Jack. Prospective Medicine. Methodist Hospital of Indiana. 1604 North Capitol Av. Indianapolis, IN 46202. 1979.

Holy Scriptures. The Jewish Publication Society of America. Philadelphia, PA 1963.

Lovell, Jim and Kluger, Jeffrey. Lost Moon. Houghton Mifflin Company. 215 Park Avenue South, New York, NY 10003. 1994

Mario Salvadori. Why Buildings Stand Up. WW Norton & Co. New York, NY. 1997

Mann, J. John, MD. A Current Perspective of Suicide and Attempted Suicide. Annals of Internal Medicine:136:4 February 19, 2002.

Murdock, Rick and Fisher, David. Patient Number One. Crown Publishing. New York, NY. 2000

New England Journal of Medicine. Aids- The First 20 Years. Vol.344, No23. pp1764-1772. June 23,2001.

Railroad Accident Report. Derailment and Collision of Amtrak Passenger Train 66 with MBTA Commuter Train 906 at Back Bay Station, Boston, Massachusetts, December 12,1990. National Transportation Safety Board.

Standard College Dictionary. Funk and Wagnalls. New York, NY. 1963.

Strong, Sanford. Strong on Defense. Simon and Schuster Inc. 1230 Avenue of the Americas, New York, NY 10020. 1996.

Survival, Evasion and Escape. US Army Field Manual. Dorset Press, Marlboro Books, Moonachie, NJ 07074.

Troebst, Cord Christian. The Art of Survival. Doubleday and Company, Garden City, NY. 1965.

The Wall Street Journal. September 6, 2000 and subsequent issues. September 11, 2001 and subsequent issues. The Wall Street Journal, 200 Liberty St. New York, NY 10281.

WEB SITES

American College of Emergency Physicians:
  www.acep.org

American Heart Association: www.cpr-ecc.org

Everyday Crisis Management:
  www.everydaycrisismanagement.com

Federal Bureau of Investigation:
  www.ifccfbi.gov

Federal Emergency Management Agency:
  www.fema.gov

Firestone: www.firestone.com

Helping: www.helping.org

Insurance Institute for Highway Safety:
  www.highwaysafety.org

Johnson and Johnson: www.jnj.com

Morgan Stanley: www.morganstanley.com

National Sagfety Council: www.nsc.org

Red Cross: www.redcross.org

Survival: www.wilderness-survival.net

United Nations Aids Group: www.unaids.org

United States Geographic Survey: www.usgs.gov

EVERYDAY CRISIS MANAGEMENT WEB SITE

www.everydaycrisismanagement.com

Go to the web-site for information on the author and the book. The site features interesting insights into how the book developed and a "behind the scenes" look at the process of writing and publishing. Information will be posted on book signings and other ways to get an autographed copy. Crisis management tips and articles on current events topics from a crisis management viewpoint will be posted. Information on contacting the author is also available on the web-site.

CONSULTING, TRAINING, SPEAKING

Dr. Mark Friedman and other experienced consultants are available for business and organizational consulting and training related to crisis management through the Medical Associates Group. Our consultants bring a unique viewpoint, in addition to many years of experience, to the task of crisis related management. To inquire about our consulting services please send email to markedoc02@aol.com or conventional correspondence to:

    Medical Associates Group
    4305 Lonetree Ct.
    Naperville, IL 60564

Speakers, including Dr. Friedman, are available for corporate and other group functions with sufficient advance notice through the Medical Associates Group Speakers' Bureau. Topics can be selected from a list of standard presentations or tailored to a specific subject or audience. Rates and availability can be queried at the above addresses.

ABOUT THE AUTHOR

Mark L Friedman MD is a 1973 graduate of the College and 1977 graduate of the Pritzker School of Medicine of the University of Chicago. In 1991-1992 he was a Kron Scholar at the Kenan-Flagler Business School of the University of North Carolina.

Dr. Friedman is a Fellow of the American College of Emergency Physicians and the American College of Physicians. He has been Chief of Emergency Medicine at St. Elizabeth's Hospital of Boston, and Assistant Professor of Medicine at Tufts University.

Currently he is Assistant Clinical Professor of Emergency Medicine at the University of Illinois at Chicago, and a practicing emergency physician.

During his business career Dr. Friedman has been President of St. Elizabeth's Emergency Medical Associates and The Brighton Group, CEO of National Medical Claims Analysts, and Vice President at Concentra Managed Care. He has been involved as a principal in entrepreneurial startups. Currently Dr. Friedman is President of Medical Associates Group.

Printed in the United States
1101800002B